'Inspirational! Essential reading for anyone wanting to follow a life of Magic and spiritual empowerment.'
ATHENA STARWOMAN ~ MYSTICAL VISIONARY AND AUTHOR

'Here at last is a user-friendly guide to practical witchcraft. Deborah Gray shows us how to gain self-empowerment by opening ourselves to the secret powers of Nature and the Goddess.'
NEVILL DRURY ~ CRAFT HISTORIAN AND AUTHOR

The Good Witch's Guide to Wicked Ways

Deborah Gray

JOURNEY EDITIONS
Boston • Tokyo • Singapore

This edition published in 2001 by Journey Editions, an imprint of Tuttle Publishing and Periplus Editions (HK) Ltd., with editorial offices at 153 Milk Street, Boston, Massachusetts, 02109.

First published by HarperCollins Publishers, Sydney, Australia, in 2001.
This edition published by arrangement with HarperCollins Publishers Pty Ltd.

Library of Congress Cataloging-in-Publication Data in Process
ISBN: 1-58290-061-2

Distributed in North America by

Tuttle Publishing
Distribution Center
Airport Industrial Park
364 Innovation Drive
North Clarendon, VT
05759-9436
Tel: (802) 773-8930
Toll free tel: (800) 526-2778
Fax: (802) 773-6993
Toll free fax: (800) 329-8885

Photographs by Stephen Oxenbury, 2C Management
Cover and interior illustrations by Sue Ninham

05 04 03 02 01   9 8 7 6 5 4 3 2 1
Printed in the United States of America

DEDICATION

My deepest thanks,

To my mother, for being my living example of the Goddess of
nurturing and unconditional love.

To my father, for showing me the importance of an
independent and searching spirit.

To my grandmother Ruth, for still astonishing us all with such
strength, wisdom and the sparkle of irrepressible youth.

To Giancarlo, my soul mate and partner, for your
never-ending support, love and mystical insight.

To my coven sister Leonora and my star companion and dear friend Athena
—thank you for your eternal support and for helping keep the Magical flame alive.

And to Helen Littleton, Katie Mitchell
and Kate Pollard, for all your patience and creativity.

And to all my past, present and future readers,
thank you for helping to make this book possible.

The brightest of blessings and love to you all!

Contents

PART TWO Magic 101 55

PART THREE Essential Witchery 129

Foreword

WELCOME, FELLOW SEEKER

You may have just started studying witchcraft and Magic, and may be looking around at all the different ways and traditions. Or perhaps you have been studying for a long time and already feel a strong connection to one particular witchy tradition or ancient path. Maybe you just want to enjoy reading about some of the old Magic arts, to add some valuable new insights to your own spiritual knowledge.

Whatever awakened your spirit and set you on your path as a seeker, and whatever brought you here to read this book, or first inspired your journey into Magic is correct and perfect for you.

Every one of us who feels the urge to remember the ancient philosophies and ways of the Wise Ones—whether or not we have been studying for a few months or years as a solitary practitioner, or have lived in a well-established and traditional coven for two or three decades, or have just started reading a few books on the subject—has the right to practice Magic and to say out loud: 'I am a witch'. And that right begins the split second our interest is sparked.

The very moment you awaken your search for Magical knowledge is the moment you conciously become a magician. That may happen when you are inspired by some great words in a book or when you look up at the sky one night, see the twinkling stars and suddenly realize with wonderful certainty and lucidity that

'Life itself is Magic'.

Many other wonderful and inspiring events can spark that conscious awakening, and it can happen at any age or stage of life.

And from that moment on, if you keep your spiritual goals in focus and keep listening to your inner voice and instincts, if you keep your mind and heart open to learning as much as you can about the mysteries and wonders of the Universe, you will be well on you way to a deeper understanding and eventually the essential practice of the beautiful and inspirational Craft of the Wise.

If you have taken the time to open your heart and mind to self-knowledge, you have already opened the first and most important of many doors—and you have already begun your wonderful journey to becoming a Real Witch.

So congratulations, fellow seeker, and welcome to the world of Magic.

The first part of this book relates to the inner lore and deeper meanings of witchcraft—what being a witch is all about. The second provides essential knowledge and secret keys to get you started as a witch, with 'How-to' instructions for spellcasting, and different tools and techniques for Magical mastery and enchantment. The third part is brimming with spells, charms and Magical cures of all kinds for you to enjoy. Any spells mentioned in the other parts of the book are given in detail in this section.

Introduction

TWILIGHT OF THE SORCERERS

During my early teen years, when I was a young witchling, taking my first steps out into the big, wide world, fate jolted me onto an amazing roller coaster ride of life experiences. Along with them came a series of prophetic visions and deep inner reflection. I then set out on a quest to find a spiritual teacher, a Merlin of Magic, who could help reawaken my heritage in the Craft and show me the true ways of the Wise.

And, for whatever reason, the God/dess must have heard me calling, because before long I became a Master's Apprentice to an Old Sorcerer, an adept philosopher of the Occult who in this life and dimension had chosen to teach in the manner of a Druid Master of Witchcraft. An exceptional being who came to feature prominently in my life as a witch.

Now, after 25 years of metaphysical study and a great response to my first spellbooks, I feel the time is here to share the secrets of my own journey into witchcraft, and to reveal more of the deeper insights and mysteries behind this timeless heritage of universal knowledge and enchantment.

I have also been inspired by the sense of special time approaching. A door of opportunity is reopening and many of us who have journeyed into the Craft and all the other Magical paths are remembering our Dreamtime Circle. We are coming back together again, and all the different old souls are feeling the sense of Gathering; in the Craft we call it the 'Quickening'. You are probably feeling it yourself.

It is a sense of an imminent Golden Age where all of us, whatever our spiritual choices, will have an incredible opportunity for clear vision, to see what's ahead and be able to take definite steps to get there. It's a Magical vision that has been seen and felt before in times past and is now being awakened within the many different spiritual tribes, including all the indigenous and pagan peoples around this planet. We are experiencing an intensification of enchanted energy, catching glimpses through the mists of time and seeing the magnificent vision of our own potential.

At this special time I have chosen to share my personal journey into witchcraft, which is a unique one, as are all spiritual journeys. Just as I found my way, you too are capable of being a great magician, sorcerer and wizard. The Magic is there inside you, just waiting to be discovered. You have the power to make it real.

Magic is real and dreams can come true.

Goddess blessings,
Deborah Gray

Congratulations, fellow seekers, and welcome to the world of magic...

witch is the way?

What's being a witch all about? — Finding your witchy way — What's wicca? — Finding a teacher or coven — some inside info (on magic, manipulation, rules and redes, demons and ghoulies) — You hexy witch — Your ancient heritage — Making natural connections — Get into a good head space — Witchy wild and free

Part One

What's Being a Witch All About?

first of all, it's a unique experience. All witches are a magically unique people and will experience their spiritual journey into Magic in their own special way and time.

I've believed in magic since the age of four, when I began casting spells for the nature spirits in my grandmother's garden. By the time I turned 18, I had managed to charm two prime ministers and become a Sorcerer's Apprentice. And while I enjoyed a successful life in public as a TV actress and singer, I was also being privately educated in the ancient mysteries and living in one of the world's best schools of wizardry and witchcraft.

I've studied and practiced the Craft for over 25 years, and now as a grown-up witchy woman and artist, I'm still on a wonder-filled and magical quest as I travel the world performing, writing and lecturing about it.

Every witch comes to the Craft in different ways and sees Magic through different eyes and cultures. But witches all over the world, in the past, present and future seem to have a shared spirit and motivation—and that is the quest for truth and knowledge.

Witches and alchemists have always known that great magical power comes to those who know how to tap into the eternal Life Force and the wisest of them also knew that the greatest power comes with attaining self-knowledge and harmony. A real witch lives a life filled with free-spirited creativity, a passionate sense of the mystical world and a boundless love for Earth and Nature. This is a Craft that is about exploring the ways of the Universe and connecting you with the infinite source of ancient wisdom and alchemy, it's about becoming a Magical Master of your own life, empowered with your own and the eternal energies of all that is, and all that has ever been.

Oh, yes and it's also about casting spells—with all of the above in mind. And what all we witches have common access to—those already practicing and all the wannabe witches-in-waiting—

is the source of real Magic.

Once you get the hang of it, and you've connected to the source of Real Magic, it becomes a part of you and a life asset that you always have with

3

you. Whatever path into the Craft you may choose, inside and out, you're a mobile Magicmaker, ready to switch on, plug into the eternal Life Force and weave your spells and charms wherever and whenever you want to.

Living with Magic is an integral part of what I do and feel every day. One of my favorite sayings is: 'If you don't believe in Magic, how can Magic believe in you?' After all, if you don't believe in yourself, how can other people believe in you? I think that it's so important for people to realize that they are spiritual and magical beings. And for me, that knowledge is one of the most powerful tools in my life. Of course, everyone is different and not everyone has the time or the inclination to learn all the techniques or study on the level that a longtime witch, shaman or even an astrologer does. But it is important that whenever something magical happens to you, something that you just know is more than a mere coincidence, that you allow your spirit to acknowledge it. Let yourself stop and feel the inspiration of that moment, where you can really say to your-self: 'Yes, that was miraculous—that was magic!'

In the study of witchcraft and metaphysics we often look back to days past and the wonderful wisdom of the ancient teachers and philosophies. But I con-sider that witchcraft is also a living and constantly evolving Craft, and through-out my life I have met modern-day philosophers, masters of metaphysics and 'living goddesses' who practice their own magical and spiritual paths in today's world and are great examples of just how possible it is to successfully apply

Magic and spirituality to our modern urban lives on a daily basis. Our lives are full of enchanted and miraculous moments, especially when we take the time to look around and really notice.

As my 'stargoddess' friend Athena often says:

'Don't just wait around for your birthday to make a wish. Why not do it every day?'

Because every day is a brand-new day of your life, with new challenges and new opportunities. I know from personal experience that once you learn to tap into the eternal Universe and your own inner power, it can really change your life.

When the
student
is ready,
the master
will appear

Finding Your Witchy Way

Throughout history, there has never been just one 'correct' or 'absolute' way of being a witch or a magician. And neither should there be. Instead, there has always been as many different views and paths as there are people seeking them.

There are many different opinions and cultures in the world, just as there are many different traditions and paths of witchcraft. But it still delights and amazes me, whenever I travel around this planet and speak with the magical elders and high masters of the many different traditions and styles of witchcraft, that many of them share my belief: just like the different tribes of the human race, Magic all comes from the same infinite and loving source, and, at its most profound level, the inner cores of all magical traditions are actually not very different after all.

Whatever path into the Craft you choose to follow is correct for you, because at its highest level, the Craft should always be a path of self-acceptance and freedom of spirit.

Beginners and experienced magicians alike, whatever age or level of practice, are all constantly feeling the Magic in their own way in a free exchange of these ancient ideas and a mutual love of the Earth and Nature.

Magic is a growing, living, metaphysical Craft, and the ways of Witchcraft are diverse, with many different styles and spiritual paths.

Witches of the new millennium enjoy a wide range of magical styles and spiritual choices that include Druidry, Wicca, Voodoo, Fairy, Asatru, Celtic, Teutonic, Eclectic, Hedgewitch, Hermetic, Strega, Egyptian Tradition, Pow Wow and Dianic, among many more.

Witchcraft as it is practiced today has come from a variety of old and ancient cultures that include Celtic, Anglo-Saxon, Nordic, Roman and Greek paganism, Hebrew, Ancient Egyptian, Asian, Native American and African. There is also a burgeoning interest in Australian Aboriginal Dreamtime traditions. And many of these paths are being woven into a dazzling tapestry of old and new practices, each of them as valid and worthy of tolerance and respect as the others.

What's Wicca?

To gain a better insight into the ways of the Craft, it is helpful to understand the different uses of the Anglo-Saxon word Wicca and how that term is often applied to today's fast-growing *Wiccan* religious/spiritual path. Basically, any type of witch can rightfully use the ancient term Wicca if they so choose, because the word simply means 'witch' in Old English terminology (some scholars also connect the word Wicca even further back in history, to the Neolithic Indo-European migration and root languages, and it can also mean 'bend' or 'wise one'). However, using the term doesn't automatically mean that a person is an initiate or follower of any of today's *Wiccan* traditions or religious practices. The *Wiccan* path is just one of numerous ways of witchcraft.

Even within the popular and widespread *Wiccan* culture, which has done much to awaken and spread positive images of witchcraft and has flourished throughout America, Britain, Australia and parts of Europe, there are now many different denominations and eclectic branches. These have grown out of the core *Wiccan* traditions, which were first created by the learned and influential Englishman Gerald Gardner in the 1940s and '50s, and redeveloped in the 1960s, '70s and '80s by other famous trailblazers and writers of the *Wiccan* style of practices, such as Alex and Maxine Sanders, Doreen Valiente, Raymond Buckland, Scott Cunningham, Silveravenwolf, Starhawk, and Janet and Stewart Farrar—to name but a few.

MY WITCHY WAY

I practice the Craft as a life path to self-knowledge and spiritual empowerment. I consider my witchy 'way' to not only be from an 'old religion', but actually from the spiritual essence—a 'high psychology' and an inner lore of a very ancient form of universal witchcraft. My style of practice wasn't originated through the 'Gardnerian' line of witchcraft. My magical teacher and early training were from a completely separate Craft lineage and my way of practice also flows though the core of both old European 'Wise' craft and Druidic thought. This 'way' is still practiced today by certain Orders of magical adepts, and to get to a level of mastery, one needs to work without any dogma or superstitions of any kind.

For instance, my Coven Master and teacher, Edgar Pielke, could trace his own German/Celtic family traditions back over many centuries and he used the term spiritual master or 'Fenris the Druid Master of Witchcraft' in the sense of a 'maestro' of this old style of practice. Because he was a spiritual and Occult adept, he was able to pass on knowledge to others, but he was very careful to point out to all his students that he didn't consider himself a leader of a religious cult or a teacher of any one 'belief system' because as he always said to us: 'What you are learning are ancient Occult techniques, a free-spirited philosophy and a way into the search for Meaning and Truth—the mastery of which is beyond just one fixed religion or doctrine.'

So which path into Witchcraft is the right one?

I'm a firm believer that 'All roads lead to Rome'...

The road you decide to travel should always be your own choice—it's an important evolution in your personal destiny, after all.

SOLITARY PRACTICE

Many witches are not initiated into any particular coven tradition, and are not necessarily a part of any defined group or religion. They may prefer instead to study and work their Magic alone, blending the different rituals and various traditions and defining their own spiritual path in their own way.

Such witches are commonly known as 'solitary practitioners', and they may practice alone simply because it is not always practical or desirable to join an established coven or to find a larger study group to meet with on a regular basis. Hedgewitch is another term for a 'solitary practitioner' and can be traced back to the old German word hagarvassa, meaning 'one who rides on the hedge and boundaries'. This symbolizes the person who guards the barriers between the material and the spiritual world, as well as the old folk tradition of the village witch who usually lived alone, in the last cottage on the edge or 'hedge' of town.

In fact, solitary practice is an old-established tradition in itself, with a long history in Europe and the British Isles.

Most solitary practitioners of the past were natural adepts who worked alone as village herbalists, healers and folk charmers. The well-documented 'kenning' or 'cunning' men and women are a perfect example of this old tradition. Some were born into a hereditary line of close-knit family groups who quietly passed down their folk traditions to a next of kin.

THE COVEN CONCEPT

Except perhaps for the ancient Druid Magical study groups way back in the pre-Christian era, and some well-hidden secret societies during 'post-pagan' times, in Europe and the British Isles it was in fact quite rare to find groups of witches being able to live together or regularly study together in one place. This was particularly true during the tumultuous years of religious superstition that existed from the 11th to the 18th century, and remained relatively the same until the 20th century, when antiwitchcraft laws slowly started being repealed in different countries around the world.

Actual (as opposed to superstitious fantasy stories) 'witch festivals' and full coven gatherings in the woods or outdoors were also uncommon throughout the last thousand years or so. Understandably so, considering the incredible difficulties it would have involved to safely organize meetings during times when witchcraft and any type of magical practice or alternative spirituality were misunderstood and thoroughly persecuted.

Nowadays we are living in a much more tolerant era and, thanks to a loosening up of philosophical and spiritual rights and a growing public awareness, witches of all kinds can gather together or practice alone and unhindered in more and more countries around the world.

The Craft in all its forms is finally becoming much more accepted and understood for the

spiritually empowering and Nature-loving path it was originally meant to be.

Finding a Teacher or Coven

Witchcraft is a working craft where you are learning to understand and work with both the known physical world and the spiritual metaphysical world. And there are different types of teachers and schools.

First, there are the 'tools and technology' teachers who usually run workshops that teach 'witch friendly' material such as crystals, astrology, tarot and palm reading, aromatherapy and herbalism. These kinds of teachers and public courses are easily found by looking in the advertising section of New Age and witchcraft magazines or by going along to the various 'mind, body, spirit' festivals that are always being held at different times and cities throughout the country. Alternatively, there are lots of good teaching books available for either beginners or advanced students that go into detail about these kinds of witchy tools and technologies.

Second, there are the spiritual teachers and the occult masters of witchcraft. These are either solitary mentors or coven leaders, and the good ones are genuine elders who are highly respected and have developed their mastery over many years (a true elder is someone with at least 15 or 20 years of experience). They are much more private and are rarely found simply by looking in the Yellow Pages.

Finding the right teacher or coven is a very personal thing.

The fact that you have to do your own search, and strive to follow your own way and instincts to find them, is an important and ancient part of the Craft process.

I've had quite a few important magical guides and mentors in my life, the very first and by no means least being my own mother and father—both of them intuitive philosophers of life who first set me on my witchy way by showing me the importance of self-knowledge and a searching spirit. They raised me with a great sense of natural wonder and respect for all things Magical and mystical.

But coming face to face with 'my Merlin' was a major turning point in my life, a truly bewitching moment. My first meeting with Edgar (Fenris—the Master Druid) was one of recognition and certainty that I was Home, where I belonged, and in the presence of a master of metaphysical knowledge and the ways of ancient mysteries and witchcraft.

While still a teenager, I had started looking further into the inner lore of witchcraft and took my first conscious step to finding a spiritual mentor by actually focusing on that very thought and putting it out into the Universe. As well as going deeper into my own Celtic heritage, I began a complete frenzy of mystical awakening as I studied astrology, the tarot and the power of crystals; practiced throwing the I Ching; and looked into yoga, meditation and the spiritual teachings of the Eastern philosophies, including Buddhism and Hinduism. It took a lot of searching and time, but when I was ready, it seemed that

the Universe was ready to provide my next important teacher and mentor of Magic.

In your own search for your witchy way, you may also want to send a thought message out to the universe for a guide or magical mentor like I did. Or you may want to find more of a study group and learn from a few different teachers. You could take witchy workshops, or get together with a circle of friends and compare magical notes and techniques. Or, if the opportunity arises, you may want to join a coven.

During the 1970s I not only joined, but also lived in a close family-like environment inside a coven house (coven-bound, some people call it). This unusual way of life doesn't suit everyone, but for me it was a wonderful spiritual foundation stone that has guided me well throughout my careers and my entire adult life, thanks to a spiritual master who was connected to an ancient way of the Craft and lovingly advised me, and our inner circle, of a true and wonderful sense of magical wisdom and alchemy. Edgar (Fenris, the Druid Master) not only taught the ancient mysteries and magic, but he also focused on ways to bring balance and harmony to our everyday lives in and out of the coven. If we ever had a coven motto, it would have been:

'Walk the middle way and keep a sense of balance'.

He taught me not to overdo anything or let the Magic ceremonies and spell-casting overshadow the work I needed to do every day on my inner self.

It was a typical, old Druidic style apprenticeship, which consists of step-by-step, one-on-one training over many years and also included the study of Magic and Occult lore, parapsychology, and the use of logic, music and poetry.

We didn't learn the Craft from a Wiccan style 'book of shadows', which was originated by the English witch Gerald Gardner, when he created the first Wiccan workbook and coven diary in the 1940s. Actually, old 'folk' traditions and earlier witches didn't keep those type of written records, as they mainly passed on the knowledge orally through the generations. But now, with a new-found tolerance and the freedom to 'come out' in the open, this contemporary method of teaching and writing down the important rituals and spells is practiced not only by Wiccan practitioners but also many other styles of witches. It has become an integral part of modern witchcraft.

My early training was from the 'mouth to ear' oral tradition of the Craft, and an emphasis on the mind/body/spirit connection, so my secret grimoire handed down through the generations is called 'the whispering book'. Edgar preferred that we commit most things to memory, which is an important part of the 'Bardic' style technique and is a great skill to learn. But as the years went on, I also started writing down much of the coven training into my own beautifully engraved spellbook, which I like to call the 'book of secrets', and some of it I've included in this book. I decided it was time to start writing down as much as I could, to make sure this information wasn't lost and could be passed on to future generations of covens and solitary witches. By the way, apart from the name 'book of shadows' or the 'book of secrets', some other witches like to call their personal diary 'the wishing book' or their 'magical grimoire'.

A GOOD APPROACH

If you choose to find a mystical teacher or coven, keep in mind that the most profound and valuable thing that even the greatest of Grand Masters and spiritual teachers can do is to help guide you to your own inner Magic and knowledge.

When you first start looking for a study group or teacher, one of the most important things to remember is not to rush it. Don't let yourself be pushed

Real Magic is taught in the spirit of love and support. Real Magic is stronger in the spirit of love and support. Real Magic is learned in the spirit of love and support. Real Magic is taught in the spirit of love and support.

into anything or feel rushed by anyone else, and that applies to all aspects of student/teacher and human relationships. Take your time.

Do your own research into what information and teachers are available, and also have a good think about whether or not you are ready for a teacher or really need one. After all, you may very well prefer to remain a solitary practitioner and

experience your Magical journey in your own way and in your own time.

And that would be absolutely your choice and a perfect decision.

You don't have to find a teacher or be initiated into any type of coven to be a genuine witch, because all the eternal knowledge and wisdom of the universe is already there inside you and may be awakened in different ways.

For instance, many people are naturally gifted, and some may have 'crossed the abyss' through extraordinary experiences and life-changing events that are in a real sense the ultimate kind of initiation into true knowledge.

Read any books that appeal to you, and that you understand and feel comfortable with. Most importantly, follow your gut instincts about people, spiritual mentors, schools, study groups, teachers, Web sites and covens.

You know that funny feeling in the pit of your stomach? Well those tummy butterflies are wise little creatures and will never steer you wrong. When they start fluttering, sit quietly and listen.

IS THIS THE RIGHT TEACHER OR COVEN?

If you do come across a potential mentor or coven, step back and observe how the mentor or coven leader is applying Magic to their own lives before you entrust them with guiding yours.

Most covens have some type of leaders, hierarchical system or high priestess/priest, and their magical purpose and direction is usually steered by the leader or leaders.

Don't be overly impressed by lofty titles alone or certificates that say 'graduate of Occult studies' or 'initiated by such and such into such and such Craft lineage'. The growing popularity of this type of certificate is a new phenomenon in the Craft, and I wouldn't recommend using them alone to judge someone's expertise as a spiritual guide.

Instead, ask yourself this series of simple and logical questions, then listen to what your inner gut voice tells you:

- Do their teachings appear to be working for them?
- Does the teacher or coven leader appear to follow their own spiritual advice and apply their knowledge and techniques successfully into their own normal everyday life?
- How many years have they been doing this?
- Do they seem to cope pretty well with the normal ups and downs of daily life?
- How does this person act when they are with you and with other people? Do they respect your decisions, personal freedom, independence and right to make your own choices?

- All teachers need to be confident and strong-willed, and may even have to be quite assertive with disruptive or noisy students. But does this person generally appear kind, tolerant and patient with you and others?

- During your magical lessons, does the coven leader or teacher answer questions well, and can they converse naturally and spontaneously about their own specialty and path? Or, if they are more of an eclectic teacher, can they speak easily about their own valuable experiences, visionary ideas and different Magical subjects?

- And, most importantly for a spiritual teacher or coven leader, do they show a well-balanced and mature perspective on life, and are they loved and respected by their students and friends?

Let's face it, there is no point in joining a circle, coven or study group where the head of the group is immature or inexperienced, can't cope with the responsibility or is someone who is unstable or stuck in a distorted view of witchcraft.

If you are confident that the spiritual mentor or high priest or priestess is both highly respected and experienced, feel free to ask him or her lots of questions before you join their circle, group or coven.

They should respect and understand your natural interest and concerns.

Some Inside Info

Before we go any further, here's some inside information, straight from the witch's mouth, to dispel some myths that surround the subject of Magic. First, are Magic spells manipulative? What's the chance of calling up a demon? When does a witch use her hexing powers? And, finally, can a man be a witch, and if so, what do we call him?

MAGIC OR MANIPULATION?

Witches have been casting love spells, making healing medicines and good-luck charms, doing astrology charts and looking into the past and future for thousands of years. We spend our whole life looking at the hidden, Occult mysteries and how the science and Magic of the universe works, and that includes bending time and space and inventing ways to cause changes within ourselves and the world around us.

24

If someone wants to classify that as manipulation, they would be at least half right. But that is the essence of witchcraft and alchemy. This is, after all, the Craft of 'bending and weaving'.

But it's our own universe we are 'bending and weaving', and we study Magic and cast our spells to help us become masters of our own lives.

For hundreds of years, there has been a myth and distorted perception that witches take over another person's 'free will' when casting a love spell or that they control other people with their Magic. That is one of the main reasons witches were persecuted in the past, and it is really a lot of superstitious nonsense left over from the Dark Ages.

A Magic spell performed correctly can certainly change the atmosphere and greatly alter the dynamic flow—the energy patterns—between two or more people, which in itself is an incredible feat.

A powerful sorcerer can 'bend' and 'weave' perceptions and dynamic energies, which in turn may have an effect on the choice another person is going to make. But that person's final decision and ultimate choice is always made according to their own free will and universal destiny, and that can't be taken away by or replaced with a spell.

Now this is where logic comes into play when working with Magic, and if you are really interested in the inner lore and High Magic of the craft, the following information is important to think about.

Our god/dess Nature endows us all with the gift of free will so that we have the ultimate choice and responsibility for our own lives. Your free will is yours alone and is one of your greatest powers. It gives you the ability to shape your own life and future.

No one else has the power to take that away from you—and you don't have the power to take it away from anyone else—not with a Magic spell or any other enchantment.

This is one of those natural laws of the universe that many people (including some witches) either misunderstand or are too caught up in superstitious beliefs to think about clearly.

Magic can't completely go outside the Laws of the Universe; it doesn't work that way, and that's not the point of the exercise.

The influence a witch has on others is fleeting, but the influence she has on herself and her own destiny is huge, and that is what a Real Witch looks for and where her greatest Magical power lies.

There are thousands of people in the world who now follow the pagan or goddess way of spiritual worship and devote their life to it as their path or religion, and there are many people among them who don't call themselves witches or cast any spells, which is completely their right and choice.

Not all pagans practice Magic and Witchcraft. And not all witches follow a pagan religion.

If someone follows certain elements of magic and the Craft but at the same time feels it is wrong or strictly against their beliefs to go ahead and use his or her acquired skills, then I also wouldn't call that person a 'witch'.

Weaving charms and casting spells is certainly a part of what witches did in the past, what they've finally got the freedom to do again, and—with a dash of luck—what we will still be doing for many millennia to come.

'Take hold of your own lives. Most of the things that distress you, you can avoid, and most of the things that dominate you, you can overthrow.
You can do what you will with them.'

Plato, 400 BC

RULES AND REDES

There are a lot of different opinions around about what is 'good' and what is 'bad' or manipulative Magic. People also speak often about the 'laws of threefold return'.

Quite a few paths within the Craft have their own rules and what they call *redes*. These are more like guides or suggestions for higher-minded behavior, and are not absolute laws of witchcraft.

Contrary to popular belief, the current forms of written redes are not from ancient religious texts and so-called 'witches' laws', or from any known ancient practice of the Craft. They are primarily a 20th-century creation.

The widely known Wiccan Rede was first set down by the influential Gerald Gardner for his own book of shadows and as a guide to his more publicly accessible magical practices around the 1940s. Since then, it has been adapted and revised many times by the leaders and spiritual writers of the different Wiccan and neo-goddess traditions that came after.

You will often see the phrases 'an it harm none, do as thou will' and 'the Law of threefold return' written into many modern books on witchcraft and Wicca. These popular phrases weren't actually derived from old writings of Celtic or British Wicca Craft; they are symbolic terms that have been adapted from a variety of different sources and cultures, including the Freemasons and Rosicrucians, Alistair Crowley and some of the Asian-based 'karmic' philosophies such as Buddhism.

Both of these terms are lovely analogies that suggest that whatever energy you send out will eventually be returned to you, and if you allow the 'intent' of your actions to be for a positive transformation, you will receive a positive outcome.

Whatever rules and redes a modern witch may choose to work under, he or she is still surrounded by the inevitable Laws of Nature.

That doesn't apply only to Magic. Every action you take in life causes not just one or threefold reactions but a myriad of effects. It's always wise to think anything through and look before you leap.

Man-made rules and religious guidelines depend on individual choices and beliefs. But if you are concerned about karma and would like to feel confident you are following a higher-minded Magic, follow these steps: Try to maintain a fair-minded and well-balanced outlook during your normal everyday life; spend time looking into your inner self and keep working to gain spiritual and emotional awareness and harmony; then the judgment you always know you can trust — is your own.

Always remember that it's best to follow your own

true will and judgment when casting your spells and charms,

because that's where most of your power comes from.

DEMONS AND GHOULIES

Don't worry, modern witchcraft is not about trying to raise up nasty demons and ghoulies. And even if you wanted to waste your time trying, you'd have more chance of flying to Mars on a broomstick than raising even a slightly cranky dust mite.

This kind of legend and bad press in witchcraft is left over from the days of religious persecution, when anyone who was even remotely an alternative thinker was labeled a heretic and thought to be invoking demons and evil spirits.

The Hollywood-style witchcraft that you see in films and teen TV shows—with all of the invoking of entities and calling up well-dressed demons (à la *Charmed*)—is great fun and very entertaining, but it's all just fantasy, the product of a scriptwriter's vivid imagination.

Throughout the many years I've spent as a witch and been practicing Magic both alone and with different Occult masters, I've found nothing to fear in the supernatural or Occult world.

Yes, of course there are many fascinating and awe-inspiring energies swirling around the metaphysical plane.

But that is also true of the 'real' physical world we live in every day and night; it too is packed full of incredible and mysterious energy. (If you've ever been to the post-Christmas sales, you'll know just what I mean.)

Everyone on the planet, not just witches, manages to live side by side and quite comfortably with a whole array of incredible energies and powers on a daily basis. In fact, most people don't think twice about it. Next time you see the sun peeking through the clouds, catch a glimpse of the ocean or watch a bolt of lightning flash across the sky in a thunderstorm, just think about how much amazing power and energy there is right here in our 'normal' lives. No wonder the Ancients gave these natural phenomena names like Thor the god of Thunder, Amon Ra the Sun god and Neptune the Lord of the Sea.

You see, what many people may think of as supernatural or 'from the otherworld' is just another dimension of the whole picture of Nature and ourselves.

So try and abandon any superstitions or fears from spellcasting and rituals. The study of Magic will allow you to open up to all the possibilities of the universe and to encourage your own human and spiritual development.

The natural universe has its own built-in protective system—an uncanny awareness of the level of your understanding and what you can and can't cope with.

Trust in it.

Your intent is like a guiding light ~ a superjet that carries your Magic to its purpose.

You Hexy Witch

Our Universe is alive with a constant ebb and flow of 'yin and yang', or positive and negative energies.

There's no doubt about it—master magicians who have studied the Laws of Nature know how to both heal and hex, and they follow their own instincts in whatever their choice of magical action.

Just as there are great benefits for all of us in the ever-changing seasons—the flow between night and day, summer and winter—there are also great benefits to be gained from embracing both your light-hearted and 'bright goddess' nature, as well as loving your strong, assertive and 'dark goddess' nature.

But there is no point in embracing all that you are and never using it to help yourself or others.

A Real Witch knows that Nature is All that Is.

It's a bit silly to think that the universe puts your magic or anything else you do into just 'positive' or 'negative' categories. That is exactly what your own free will and instincts are for—to give you the choice and ability to make your own judgments.

Recently, I've seen a lot of Web sites and read many books on the Craft that happily talk all about our luscious and witchy 'dark goddess' nature, but then the material falls short on explaining how or when to use it, or curiously advises that it's not 'good' to use these powers for spellworking. On the other hand, many people may read about the 'neutral' path of a real witch and get confused when they are told that there is no such thing as a 'white witch'.

First, let me clear up some of the confusion about the term 'white' or 'good' witch'. There is a long, illustrious history of respected Craft healers who liked to call themselves 'white witches' after the ancient 'White Goddess' or 'White Lady Moon', and often because they wanted the public and any outsiders to clearly understand the *intent* of their magic. But of course, those magicians knew about the balance of nature, and they also had the ability to hex. They understood all aspects of their power to help others and themselves whenever it was needed, and this thriving old 'white' healing craft still continues today in many countries around the world. By definition, the term 'white witchcraft' certainly does include all the shades and colors of the rainbow, but I still always have a little chuckle (oh, let's face it, sometimes a really big cackle) whenever some novice magicians want to know what on earth could make me such a 'good' witch. Luckily I've had a fair bit of experience at actually living the full-on life of a witchy woman and I know for sure that no matter what fads may come and go, I am always going to be 'good' at what I do—especially when I feel like being very, very naughty.

You see, it's all about your intent and knowing where and when to use your different powers of enchantment and God/dess energies.

To put it really simply, once a real witch has done enough work on shedding some 'light' on her inner self and she knows that her instincts are honed and ready, she gains an enormous sense of her own magical power. She's learning to love all aspects of her nature, including bringing some healing energy in and out of the shadows, so she knows when it feels right to heal or hex, strike or stroke, and pretty much do what her own magical free will and intuition tell her.

Your intent is like a guiding light – it's a superjet that carries your Magic to its purpose.

"A magical master" can still do all of this fun stuff I like to call 'voodoo therapy' or 'sorcery for stress' without feeling uptight about it, because their magical decisions are always based on a balanced view of the situation, and it's really all about the good intent, like self-defense, honoring and resolving grief, healing yourself or others (or just 'cause it feels so damn good to let it all out and be incredibly wild and wikid for a day).

And of course, a good ol' belly laugh never hurt anyone and is especially helpful in blowing away the cobwebs of bitterness to bring closure and magically dissolve leftover anger and sadness.

WITCH OR WIZARD?

You have probably heard the saying 'there is a little bit of witch in every woman'. Well, that is absolutely right—and there are a few gorgeous goddesses thrown in for good measure too. Every woman has been equipped since birth with feminine intuition and witchy goddess power. These are natural instincts that directly align with a woman's highly developed emotional awareness and the necessary 'all-seeing' eye of a future mother and elder.

But let's not forget the males of the species, who are also called 'witches'. ('Warlock' is a misunderstood name and is rarely used these days.) Men sometimes—well, often, actually—get the short end of the stick when it comes to recognition of their own natural sensitivities, intuition and power. Being a female witch who has studied with a real live Man of Magic and met some very sensitive and intuitive male witches, I definitely consider that Witchcraft is not nor has ever been an exclusively female domain. Men and women are equal in the practice of the Craft. We need to accept and love male energy as part of the important duality and natural laws of life. Without it, true Magic is only half as effective. Just as a man needs to discover and strengthen his feminine and nurturing side, a woman gains power by discovering and strengthening her maleness and assertive masculine energy.

There is duality, male and female, yin and yang, black and white, positive and negative, in everything.

I've included a number of spells in the god and goddess section that can help empower you with the strong warrior and passionate male energies, as well as align you with both the yin and yang, male and female aspects of the Universe.

When it comes down to it, however, your ancient heritage is far more important than your chromosomal makeup in the world of Magic.

Whatever awakened your spirit and set you on your path as a seeker and whatever first inspired your journey into Magic is correct and perfect for you.

Whatever awakened your
spirit as a seeker and
set you on your path and
whatever first inspired
your journey into Magic
is correct and perfect for you

Your Ancient Heritage

Real Witches don't worry too much about certificates of Craft lineage or whether or not they had a Gypsy grandmother way back when.

Every one of us on this planet is a magical and spiritual being. We are all born with a magical heritage and a direct link to the Ancient Ones. Because you are an Ancient One—an eternally evolving soul moving through lifetimes—remembering, changing and remembering again.

Amid the diversity, there seems to be one common connection between all traditions and paths into Magic and witchcraft, and that is the feeling of a deep spiritual connection to the old Wise Ones, and our respect and admiration for them, their knowledge and wisdom, and their spellcraft.

'Listening' to your dreams can be a great way of keeping in touch with your 'old' soul.

39

My own ancient self is never very far away during sleep and waking hours, and sometimes it actually jumps right out and takes me by the hand into my past lives. When I first started working on this book, I started having a strong 'vision' dream. I was out on a great plain sitting next to a fire in the misty, cold night air. When I looked around I saw that I was part of a big circle consisting of old grandmothers and younger women of all different races. Next to me were old Native American grandmothers, as well as Caucasian, African and Asian women, and what appeared to be a number of fur-clad women of Eskimo descent. I had this dream for a few nights in a row, but the very last night I had it, one of the women stood up and crossed over the circle to me and gave me a warm hug, as if we'd known each other for a long time. Then we said goodbye with the words: 'Sister, we'll meet again through the mists of time.'

A couple of days later I was on the internet, holding a live chat with the members of my virtual magic circle, when, as often happens, a brand-new member came online and started to introduce herself. This in itself was not at all unusual, but for some reason my heart started pumping loudly when I saw the name 'Delfina Rose, Native American Shamaness' written on the computer screen. For a split second I was transported to that same dream circle of magical women. As I came back again—a heartbeat later—to 'real time', I read her message. She spoke about her Native American Shaman and Irish background and stories of her own circle of elders, including the grandmothers in her tribe. I felt my ancient self and my inner voices singing so loudly to me that I took the very unusual step of asking this 'virtual' stranger to contact me off-line, to see if she had picked up any similar 'voice' callings and vibrations.

Delfina, being the Shamaness and experienced magician that I have since found her to be, also had absolutely no doubts that our 'accidental' meeting was something of great meaning to us both—especially since she'd had a similar vision a while before. We have since spoken about what this reawakening means and have both done separate rituals to go back and meet ourselves again—to help us discover the project we set for ourselves all those eons ago. Now that the mists are lifting, the time is here; we are planning to do some type of project together and will meet, most probably in her healing center in Arizona. Whatever work our ancient selves have in mind for us, we will incorporate much of our dual visions and training with our elders into some type of joint mission. This seems to be just one of the many tasks my ancient self has already set down for me to do, both alone and with other old souls.

Many witches today want to follow a similar spiritual path to the Ancient Magicians, and many of us either have 'memories' or a strong sense of what the Old Ones knew and understood.

For some of us, it may even seem like a re-awakening of our old training.

For those of us who believe in the eternity of the spirit, there is the follow-on logic that a naturally adept practitioner of Magic could simply be carrying on his or her role and path from a previous lifetime.

In the quantum world—which the old alchemists and witches knew about and worked with long before the word was even invented—and using meditation techniques and through experience, you may start to find that there is no difference between past, present and future.

You may come to understand that anyone can instantly connect with and access these ancient ways of knowing.

In other words, you can learn to bend time and space, to travel to other dimensions and be instantly connected to an old Druid as he walks you—his apprentice—through an ancient Irish grove, or be sitting in a philosophy class listening to Plato himself, or spend a few hours in a Hermetic School of Magic.

And, who knows, you may even be able to plug into the actual thoughts and living memories of that ancient philosopher or master magician.

In Magic, nothing is impossible! It is really just a matter of spending time learning and applying the natural laws of the universe on a daily basis.

We are the ancestors. We are the Wise Ones. We retain the living memories of them, as we learn how to remember.

Some people actually have flashbacks of who they were in a past life, and there are spells and rituals you can perform to help get a clearer view of your previous incarnations (I've included one in Part Three).

There are other ways, too, to connect with your ancient knowledge, which is a big part of what being a witch is all about.

THE RE-AWAKENING PROCESS

Learning the first steps in Magic is really a re-awakening to what your spirit already knows. That is why you have been attracted to it, because your spirit recognizes it and feels familiar—at home—with this knowledge and way of looking at life.

The paradox is that this knowledge is never exactly the same for each person. We don't have to reinvent the wheel, because it is all there for us to access in these ancient philosophies and spiritual paths.

But during the natural evolution process, you do add your own unique perceptions and consciousness to this ancient wisdom. And through you a new way of understanding and, eventually, imparting this knowledge may be born.

This is the way that knowledge evolves naturally and is passed on to future generations. But every Witch will follow these steps in his or her own unique way and time.

'All that has been will be again but never the same.'

Fenris, the Master Druid

The Three Stages

There appear to be three clear stages involved in attaining magical knowledge that, given enough time and study, most Witches will go through.

- The first stage involves recognizing your latent and natural ability. This includes the initial years spent searching for a suitable path, guides, spiritual teachers or apprenticeship.
- The second step occurs in the middle years, which are spent in continuous study and daily application of the magical knowledge as you grow and mature.
- The third step is where you reach a level of maturity and mastery in your path. In this stage you naturally become a cocreator and may wish to teach or to find some other way to pass the knowledge that you have acquired on to others.

But to begin with, more about setting that whole wheel in motion.

Making Natural Connections

When I was just a young kid, several years before I joined a Druid's Circle, I began searching for ways to keep awakening and strengthening my inner Magic. And one of the best ways that I found was to spend a lot of time in nature and to take the time to really look at the beautiful world around me. You see, being a Witch and applying your Magic is not just about specific techniques or rituals and defined doctrines, rules and redes. It is really a spiritual way of life, an inner journey, where you are learning to know and understand yourself, and to see the world around you for the truly magical and miraculous place it is.

I vividly recollect the time I spent in my grandmother's garden as a small child. It was a carefully tended English garden—a paradise of old world scents, of lavender and roses. It backed onto a national park where I explored hidden mossy caves and swam in freshwater streams along with slippery tadpoles. I was surrounded by an abundance of almost fluorescent native bushflowers, wild mushrooms and smelly, sticky toadstools—all of which I put to magical use, pulling them apart and mixing and mushing them to make strange potions used in secret rituals for the many sprites and fairies I communed with daily.

Through my natural childlike wonder and innocence, I discovered an important truth of witchcraft: that even though certain rituals and ancient techniques are valuable to learn and important to know, the most basic, simple things—such as sitting or lying under a tree (they don't call us 'tree huggers' for nothing), feeling its energy and life force and connecting with the earth under your body and feet—are a vital part of it.

Doing this can begin to align you with some of the natural laws of Magic as well as the wonderful Elements such as Earth.

Remember the old expression 'knock on wood'? This comes from old magicians, like the Druids, who would knock on an oak tree to contact the tree spirits.

Being outdoors, feeling the soft breeze on your face and practicing deep-breathing techniques and meditation can directly align you with the element of Air; doing so on a beach or in the sun aligns you with Water or Fire.

If you'd like to perform magic rituals to get in touch with the natural elements Earth, Air, Water or Fire, I've given you the guidelines and incantations for each in Part Three of this book. Using them, you can align yourself with the chosen element and be able to invoke the solidness of the earth beneath you, the lightness and freedom of the breeze, the might of the seas, or the vitality of the sun, for example.

You will find that the more you practice these simple rituals, the more connected with your inner Magic and that of the universe you become.

The most simple and natural things in life are usually the most profound and Magical.

Your spirit is eternal and is connected with all knowledge and wisdom in the universe. Your own mind and body contain the same elements as the stars, the planets, the ancient cosmic dust, as well as the elements and memories of all intelligence and genius, all that has ever been and will ever be—past, present and future.

47

Get Into a Good Head Space

A real witch should be well read and mentally active—after all, it's our mind that really does the focusing and application of true Magic. So you should be constantly exercising, training and strengthening your brain power. The more you train your mind, the better a magician you become. And that includes practicing both creative and logical thinking.

A witch should never become 'one-eyed', or stuck in one point of view. You should be able to see the many different facets in everything—in people, opinions and everything around you.

Paradoxes are everywhere. Whatever truth you discover, the opposite is also true.

Read and learn about as many different philosophies and histories as you can. Don't learn just about Wicca or Druids, witches and spellcasters. Look into both modern and ancient science. Read the ancient Greek classics and Roman legends, and the writings of ancient philosophers and great minds of the past. Investigate the modern psychologists and visionaries such as Carl Jung and Joseph Campbell as well.

It's a step-by-step process, and even after 10, 20 or 30 years of study, you'll find that the most important step is to keep learning to know yourself and look at the world and others in a nonjudgmental and loving way. If you can do that, then most other processes will follow naturally at their own pace and in their own time.

Once you begin to understand the inner meaning of the rituals and various forms of practice, you will actually begin to go beyond the more set and defined forms and techniques and into the higher source of the Craft.

One of the strange paradoxes you can't help but find when studying the ancient lores of Magic is that the more you become aware of the deep psychology and forgotten meanings behind these old rituals and ancient practices, the more you see just how mutable, flexible and alive in the here and now the core of it really is. It can be as fresh and new for us as it was when our ancestors first discovered these magical techniques many thousands of years ago.

This is why I'm not averse to the ways of the Craft moving out of the broom closet—I don't have any fear of it losing its mystery and wonder to me or others, because the more I learn, the more mysterious and magical it all becomes. The knowledge actually helps you to appreciate the mystery and enchantment of everything—not just the spells and rituals, the 'high ceremonial' part of it, but also the everyday, mundane, simple things in life; they all become a part of the great Magic ceremony of being alive.

It's wondrous, and no matter how long you study, you can never get bored because there is so much more to know. Your mental ability expands and your over-all tolerance level rises so you find that you *want* to know and keep learning more.

You'll probably find that you become addicted to reading books as well. So don't say I didn't warn you! Every mature-age witch I know is an incredible hoarder of information and usually has a collection of books—old and musty and brand-spanking new—that would make the National Library jealous.

The learning never ends. Even if you eventually become a teacher of Magic, you will remain a lifelong student. I look at my father, for instance, who was one of my first spiritual teachers. At 70 he is having another fresh burst of mental activity and mind expansion, which is truly amazing. He's writing a book trilogy based on his own theory of the meaning of life and is still looking at the world through the eyes of a young discoverer. It's a great thing to look forward to. If we start early, we witches can look forward to many years of wonder and passion in life.

The more you study through ancient wisdom, the more you see the Universe through the eyes of a child.

See Part Three for the Cosmic Awakener, which will help open up your power of mind and let you embrace the free-spirited witch within.

The elixir of magic is freedom,
And there lies a key to its alchemy for you.
Try and lock its golden light into just one box – and it instantly disappears from view.

Witchy Wild and Free

Trying to fit witchcraft into just one pathway is too narrow a concept for any Master Magician or Real Witch.

Just like Mercury, the ancient god Hermes who is Magic's favorite son, Magic and witchcraft are by their very nature wild, free, slippery and hard to pin down. And most witches are also freedom-loving individuals with strong natural spirits—they are as wild and untameable as any birds in the forest or lions in the jungle.

We are gypsies, with questioning minds and independent souls, though we may choose to stay and sit around the fire for a time, absorbing the wisdom of a spiritual master.

And we may study and respect different magical techniques and follow ancient guidelines and teachings—we don't need strict doctrines and religious dogma to show us what real Magic is. For we are already 'One' with the Universal god/dess and feel a great love for the natural world around us.

The essence of Magic is inspired through a free and unhindered spirit. It is being able to let your spirit roam where it wills, feel what it wills, be what it wills. The secret of Magical Mastery is to do the above within a well-balanced and observant perspective.

This is a spiritual path as well as a philosophy, a way of looking at science, mathematics, nature and the universe. To many, it is also their choice of religion.

All combined, it is an ancient path, but it is also a path of modern knowledge that can help us understand and walk right into the future, to look into what we and future generations on earth are going to be facing.

To be a Real Witch is an ever-evolving spiritual path that travels side by side with science, our physical health, our environment on earth, as well as our healthy sexuality and artistic expression.

It's about becoming a renaissance person and all-around human being capable of understanding and handling anything you set your mind to and, very importantly, allowing your neighbor the freedom to do the same.

Before we go on to the next chapter, here is another 'crafty' secret I'd like to reveal to you. You can all be the brightest of stars because every one of us is living in an enchanted paradise of golden opportunities. You're overflowing with so many wonderful gifts that the angels had to put them all in a cosmic bank for you. Now, on the next pages, I'd like to give you some more enchanted keys to help open up that heavenly deposit box of yours so you can really start making withdrawals from the endless well of Power and Magic.

magic
101

All you need to know to get started—

How does a spell work?—

Magical tools—

Chants and incantations—

Casting a circle—

Your indoor temple—

What's in a name?—

Magic ways and means—

Crystal power—

Magic moments, seasons and times—

Part Two

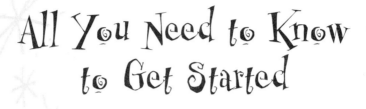

All You Need to Know to Get Started

Now that I have shared some of my magical training and given you some thoughts on what being a Real Witch is all about, I would like to show you what I know to be some of the essential tools and 'secret' keys to spellcasting and Magic.

Of course, there are many other tools and methods in the Craft, but the following techniques are designed to give either a novice magician or an experienced Crafter some tried-and-true and unique hints as well as a way into the type of magical practice that has seen me through thick and thin and produced some spectacular results for both me and my inner circle over the years. Within this section you will also see the continuing 'practical and mystical' theme I spoke about earlier, and this is to help you absorb the fact that the most successful sorcery is always done with a combination of the mystical, esoteric themes, and the actual, physical action.

A great piece of witchy advice I would like to give you is: If you can use even some of these magical essentials, along with getting actively involved in your everyday work and relationships with the same type of 'get up and go', then the world can really be your enchanted oyster.

How Does a Spell Work?

Rituals and Magic spells are beautifully creative events that can be as overtly ceremonial and theatrical or as simple and direct as you desire them to be.

Whatever style of ceremony you choose, a spell needs to be as workable in the physical world as it is in the metaphysical. I like to use a combination of Occult techniques, depending on what type of spell I intend to cast. But whichever I choose, I always take into account the environment around me and what methods can be applied to the space I am working in.

For example, I might be out of broomsticks and want to work some Magic on a jet plane as I'm flying over the two hemispheres, or I might want to connect with the elements in the middle of a desert with no tools except my own 'skyclad' body and willing mind, the earth firm beneath my feet, and the heavens soaring above me!

An excellent ritual I have for both such occasions is called 'the Universal Compass' and you can use it any time and anywhere to help you connect with the major elements and all the directions of the world.

Not only does a Magic spell work by intent and the power of your thoughts, the alignment of your body, mind and spirit is also important to its effectiveness. All three of these aspects of yourself can be brought together by:

- deep breathing and meditation;
- letting go of nervous desire and impatience; and
- being consciously aware of your connection to the eternal universe.

Don't just believe it can happen, know it and see that it already has.

All aspects of the universe, including yourself—your mind, body and spirit—are connected; we are all energy. Everything we see around us is the physical manifestation of thought, and your thoughts have the power to change the atmosphere of your mind, which can in turn change the dynamic of the atmosphere around you.

Nothing is ever destroyed or disappears entirely – everything is energy, and energy can only be transformed.

To create the right environment within and around you before a spell is cast, cleanse your aura and the space or room you will be using for spellcasting. This can be done very simply by spending some quiet time alone and calming your energies through meditation and deep-breathing exercises. If possible, you can bathe or take a shower to help wash away built-up stress.

You might like to perform your rituals 'skyclad' (what we witches call being naked). At other times you might want to wear a special robe that you only use for magical workings. What's best is to wear what feels the most comfortable and right for you.

Magical Tools

Most Magic charms use tools like candles, crystals, aromatic oils and herbs and spices, as well as spoken words and incantations. Why?

You can use these magical tools for both practical uses—as a source of light or heat, for their medicinal qualities, or to assist focus and concentration—and because each herb, color, scent and incantation has its own esoteric use and unique vibration—a magical resonance that enhances the power of your spell, just like a musical instrument enhances a song.

Imagine when playing a guitar, for instance, a particular string is plucked and gives off a particular note—a wave of energy that you not only hear, but *feel* physically and emotionally as well. When the strings are strummed together in a chord, the different notes merge and *create energy that enriches the atmosphere and causes a shift of emotions in people who are close by.*

In the same way, because we are living in a quantum universe of overlapping space and time, you can also affect the objects or persons you are focusing your Magic on, no matter how far away they are on the planet.

The esoteric vibrations of colors, for example, are commonly used in Magic. Using a red candle in a spell, for instance, suggests passion and energy, while a blue candle inspires tranquillity and peace. A complete list of candle colors and their esoteric meaning appears on the following pages. The same applies to herbs and incense that can be used in spells. If you want to bring on prosperity, for example, you could use nutmeg or sage, or if your spell or ritual has a purifying intention, eucalyptus, vanilla or thyme could be used. Following is a comprehensive list of herbs and incense and their esoteric meanings.

CANDLE COLORS
AND THEIR ESOTERIC MEANING

BLUE: success, peace, tranquillity and protection

BROWN: animal Magic, environment and grounding

GOLD: the Sun, wealth and royalty

GREEN: luck, growth, prosperity and healing

ORANGE: creativity, health and attraction

PINK: love, friendship, femininity and gentleness

PURPLE: spirituality, psychic ability and enchantment

RED: passion, lust, energy, vitality and strength

SILVER: mysticism, the Moon and prosperity

WHITE: truth, purity, meditation and spiritual protection

YELLOW: concentration and mental ability

HERBS, SPICES AND INCENSE AND THEIR ESOTERIC MEANING

ALLSPICE: spiritual vibrations and strengthens any ritual

BASIL: wealth, love and fertility

BAY: protection, clairvoyance and good fortune

CARNATION: healing, vitality and friendship

CINNAMON: luck, love and prosperity

CLOVE: memory, eyesight and attraction

EUCALYPTUS: healing and cleansing

FRANKINCENSE: high Magic, protection and purification

GARDENIA: arousing, aphrodisiac and passion

GARLIC: banishing and protection

JASMINE: spiritual love, happiness and erotic feelings

JUNIPER: safety, protection, love and affection

LAVENDER: attraction, sexuality, beauty and purification

MARJORAM: happiness, cleansing and affection

MINT: clear sight, energy and cleansing

MUGWORT: protection and powerful goddess energies

NUTMEG: prosperity, attraction and
clairvoyance

ORANGE: harmony and a happy atmosphere

ROSE: love, passion and friendship

ROSEMARY: purification, healing,
good fortune and high Magic

SAGE: prosperity, cleansing and good health

SANDALWOOD: mental ability, meditation
and tranquillity

THYME: clairvoyance, protection and purification

VANILLA: purity, affection and
feminine attraction

Chants and Incantations

When casting a Magic spell, your own voice and the words you speak are a very important part of the ritual, especially since your voice triggers certain vibrations and resonances in the universe. The old Celtic Druids and Bards considered poetry, music and the spoken word to be full of great sorcery and spent many years honing their skills in wordcraft and songs—which might explain why so many of us witches are creative writers and singers.

On the pages that follow are a few of the simple incantations I have used over the years. Some of them were passed down to me from my Elders, and I created the others. They have worked very well for me, so please feel free to use them as often as you need.

When you get a feeling for the way the structures and rhythms of the incantations work, add your own lines and use them to practice with.

After a while you will begin to see the deep connections and high Magic behind the wordcraft, poetry and music.

It really is inspiring and lots of fun, and the more you practice it, the better you become.

THE RHYTHM OF LIFE

Through my 'Bardic' family background and Druidic training, I've come to discover quite a few handy secrets about the magical ways of words, rhythms and even song melodies.

Getting to know how different word and music rhythms can cause different effects in spellcasting can take quite a bit of time and study, but here are some important keys to the understanding of it, and if you practice with these types of rhythm techniques,

you won't be a 'slave' to the rhythm, but a Magical master of it.

There are a variety of styles to enchanted rhythms. The first one is the one-liner; this is an ancient single-beat 'power stroke' that can be used on its own as a spell, or can be added to the end of a longer spell to give power and resolution. In modern terms, you could say that this is the 'pay-off' line, and interestingly enough, the one-liner is the style that's often used in modern affirmations and even commercial advertising. (There may very well have been some witchy minds working overtime when someone came up with the great power stroke of 'Share the Spirit' for the incredibly successful Sydney Olympics.)

But for our purposes, we can use magical one-liners such as the tried and true 'power strokes': 'It *Will* Be So' or 'So *Mote* It Be' or the slightly longer 'So *Shall* My Request Be Heard'. Note that there is an emphasis on the action words in the line to help push the rhythm along.

The most popular of the incantations are the rhyming kind that usually have about three or four lines. The words will tell a little story about the type of spell it is and the intent or purpose of the charm.

For instance, you can probably guess instantly the intention of the spell below, even without me explaining it to you. Note the all important pay-off line at the end that signifies the intent and purpose of the spell.

'This candle is my burning love
As bright as the sacred Sun,
May this flame warm your soul
And let us soon be one.'

The above spell is in a 4/4 rhythm, which is a popular and joyous rhythm used to enhance an incantation or a magical song. You can also play around with 3/4 rhythms, which are more waltzy and can be more poignant too. It is said that the ancient High Priestesses of Delphi also made great use of all rhythms and music for sorcery—especially the 3/4 and 4/4 beats—to get everyone excited and inspired.

You don't always have to use poetry or rhyming words to be effective. Sometimes you can use just a few very meditative or strong lines that get your point across and are more like affirmations.

*'Let all impurities be cast from me
with this cleansing breath.'*

Then you can add a more resolving power stroke line with something like:

'O Blessed Be' or 'Thank you, my Goddess'

And finally, here is a very old key to effective bardic spells and chants that has been used for many centuries—the use of the magical Quatrain. This is where you do a four-liner, and then add an extra power stroke and pay-off line at the end—sending your incantation and final intent zooming off into the Universe.

Here's an example of it that I used for a spell called the Cheapskate Charm, which appeared in *Nice Girl's Book of Naughty Spells*. (I've since heard from many readers who have had great success with this one!)

'While money is owed to those who wait,
Bills pile up and confusion reigns,
Your conscience shall prick
When I repeat this plea,
Allow what is mine to return to me.'

READYMADE INCANTATIONS

To Awaken Love For Yourself

'I now let go of unhappiness and stress
and I open my mind, body and spirit
to receive the wisdom of the Universe.'

or

'I am content in my own Universe,
I create and give love and friendship
and I will learn to know my inner self.'

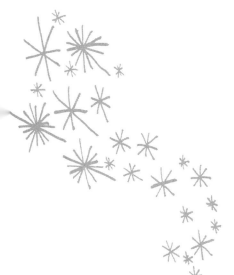

To Attract a Soulmate

Concentrate on the moon or a star
that attracts your attention and think loving thoughts.

'With these Magic words I begin my spell
Hear me, oh mystic star, hear me well.
Let your Magic light send me the love of my life.'

To Bring Back an Ex-lover

Picture yourself and this person back together
and happy again.

'Each time you wake,
each road you take,
you shall be feeling my love.'

For Getting a Job or Success in Business

'I feel it, trust it and I shall be it,
Now luck and good fortune shine on us all.'

For Peace and Harmony

'Love before me,
love beside me,
love behind me,
bring peace, harmony and truth.'

To Expel Bad Luck and Negative Energy
'All the bad energy is now gone,
I see reflected only pure light and affection.'

To Boost Self-esteem
'Deep within me, my soul is my guide,
I shall put away my fears and know
that I deserve to love and be loved.'

For Help With Legal Problems and Court Cases
'Spirit of success and justice
surround me with good fortune.'

To Heal a Broken Heart
'Oh shimmering star,
weave your magic spell tonight.
Help me feel my soul within,
so my wonderful new life can now begin.'

SONG OF KULLERONE
(SUNG IN THE KEY OF E MINOR)

If you are musically inclined, writing chants and poetry is a great way to stimulate your songwriting too. Here is an example of one of my own compositions that was written for a mystical rock opera, about a lost enchanted island called Kullerone.

"Fair maiden waiting, gold rings in her hair, her heart is breaking
White knights are riding, a sword in their hand,
Their last stand for Kullerone,
Sorcerer weaves his way into their soul,
Memories will fade
Lovers are weeping while legends are made on the shores
Of Kullerone,
Island alone, I hear you calling
O come take me home,
My Kullerone.

Put out to sea in boats made of pearl
Hear the winds howl
Sail far from the land where Magic was born
Away from our own.

Our Kullerone
Island alone, we hear you calling
O come take us home,
Kullerone.
(REPEAT ABOVE CHORUS)
O my beth, O my shay,
no traces or a sign,
you shall remain between the ways,
'Til I come to make you mine."
(WHISPER ABOVE CHANT UNTIL FADE)

Deborah Gray, 1983

75

Learning the first steps in Magic is really a re-awakening to what your spirit already knows.

Casting a Circle

When you cast a circle, you create your own magical environment and a focus of cosmic power within and around you.

Whether you cast a circle, a square, pyramid or star, you are not creating a shield or barrier from outside forces. You are creating a psychological space that can help take you out of the 'normal' mundane world that you interact with every day, and into the mystical, metaphysical world.

You don't perform circle 'boundary' rituals to switch off or block spiritual energies. You do it because you are trying to join, connect and be one with the infinite energies.

APPRECIATING
THE LAW OF THE PARADOX

What I am about to tell you next is very important to your practice as a witch and is in accordance with ancient Occult knowledge and High Magic techniques.

If it doesn't make a lot of sense to you at first, don't worry; just take the next piece of information in and know that when you are ready, its meaning will become clear.

Every action we do and experience in life has more than one meaning and more than one outcome and reaction.

An experienced witch works with the knowledge of both the physical and the metaphysical world, and we also work with the knowledge of the paradox—which exists in *both* the physical and the metaphysical worlds.

The paradox of the circle ritual and the 'boundary' you are creating is that at the same time as you are creating a circle boundary, you are also creating a circle of 'no boundaries'. You are listening with both your conscious and subconscious mind to the universal mind, which also exists in a space of 'no boundaries'.

RAISING POWER

Many witches always cast a circle or a spiral to help focus and raise energy before they begin a spell, but this is not essential practice. What you choose to do depends on your own instincts and traditions.

There are countless ways to raise energy. Some traditions cast their circle by calling up the four elements and the 'Watchtowers', and then may raise up a 'cone of power', while others believe in calling on protective spirits or angelic energies. Others again like to work with fairy or 'Faery' energies or Nature sprites or the different pantheons of ancient gods and goddesses.

Whatever methods you use, work at your own pace and try out different approaches one at a time to see what works—what resonates magically for you. What works for you will often depend on what type of person you are. Maybe you are more of a cerebral type of person who feels more inspired by being alone or sitting in a circle with others, quietly focusing your mind and body with meditative rituals. Or you may get a lot of excitement and magical value from trying out the more physically involving rituals, which can incorporate dancing, beating drums, singing and chanting (which can be done both alone or with a magical group).

The point is there is no 'right' or 'wrong' way to connect with the source of Magic and to raise up energy –

the only right thing is whether you are getting inspired from the ritual and feeling it happening.

Especially when you are just starting out in the Craft, it's best to work with rituals that inspire you in a more positive and uplifting way as well as those that help you connect with the oneness of yourself and the eternal universe.

Begin with rituals you relate to and understand. There's no point in attempting ceremonies that are so full of complicated symbols and language that you don't really know what you're trying to do and lose sight of what you are trying to achieve.

Remember to trust in the Universe so you can be fully open and relaxed. There's far less chance of you getting in touch with your witchy nature if you are fearful or cast your circle thinking you need to protect yourself from entities or 'outside forces'. Putting up psychological barriers will only create unwanted tension, and that won't allow you to fully connect or achieve anything much at all, except perhaps to give yourself a stress headache, which ain't too magical.

Even if you don't have a more experienced person to perform rituals with, you can always get in touch with your own 'wise wizard' inside yourself.

You can help dissolve any fears and tensions by performing really simple meditation and de-stressing spells, and then just take your time feeling comfortable with whatever you are doing. Don't worry, you can't hurt yourself or raise up any unwanted energies just because you accidentally say something backwards or don't do something at the perfect time—the universal energies don't ever judge you like that.

CIRCLE OF LIGHT

This wonderful ritual is one of my favorite ways of casting a circle and raising a spiral of energy. It is for focusing and invoking a sense of growth, attraction and abundance. It can help put you into a meditative and responsive state wherever you are, and

connect your spiritual and physical energies to the Universal forces around, above and below you.

It requires no external tools, but is still one of the most powerful and ancient rituals you can do. Perform it day or night, including whenever you feel your psychic and physical energies need a boost or to enhance the power of a spell.

Find a comfortable and private space, either outdoors or indoors, and stand breathing calmly. Loosely cup your hands together in front of you so that you can see the palms of both of your hands. Look closely at the center of both of your hands and look at the tiny lines on your palms. Observe how there appears to be a curved space that is perfect for holding a small sphere.

Keep looking until you visualize that small sphere softly glowing in your hands, and in your mind's eye, imagine that it contains a miniuniverse that is shimmering with thousands, then millions, of tiny suns and stars, which are starting to merge into a minigalaxy of light. The more you look into this cosmic sphere, the more you really see this miniuniverse, which has its own galaxy of stars circling slowly around inside it in a clockwise direction.

Feel the power and energy of that minigalaxy as it starts to spiral up through your entire body. When you are feeling uplifted and revitalized, start turning on the spot to the right, in a clockwise direction. Spin once or twice in a circle and joyously fling the light sphere away from you and watch the sphere dissolve into the atmosphere, scattering those thousands of tiny stars to surround you with your own expanding galaxy and circle of light.

WHY CLOCKWISE, OR 'DEOSIL'?

In the above spiral of power you turn to the right because it's an ancient symbol and psychological trigger for going forward and moving toward the light. Think about the old saying 'putting your right foot forward' and why in most cultures we greet each other by shaking the right hand. Even our clocks, our precious time keepers, turn to the right, and no matter where you are on Earth, if you stand facing the north at dawn, the first life-giving rays of the Sun will rise in the east and shine on your right side.

'Deosil' is from the old Scottish term *'Deiseal'*, meaning 'turning to the right' and is also a Craft term for clockwise or 'sunwise'. Because the Sun's energy gives us light and life, while the Moon is a cold and mysterious planet with a dark side, humans, plants and most other living creatures naturally turn toward the sunlight to 'wake up', grow and blossom. The left side, turning in the opposite direction toward the Moon and night, helps us dream, rest and travel through the more mysterious side of us. Through both evolution and culture, this 'sunwise' and 'moonwise'—right and left action—became a very strong part of the belief system. Throughout Europe and in many other parts of the world, right-turning, clockwise rituals like the one above have been performed for thousands of years and are magically effective in the most universal and profound way.

There are some left-handed and Southern-Hemisphere witches who prefer casting 'forward motion' and 'attraction' circles in a counterclockwise 'widdershins' direction. And, hey, that is perfectly cool if it works for them, but I personally wouldn't recommend you cast a forward circle in a counterclockwise direction, regardless of what country or hemisphere you might be working in. Not because anything drastic can happen, but simply because our genetic and psychological adherence to these left and right actions is often too ingrained, and it can get confusing to swap around.

COUNTERCLOCKWISE RITUALS

The left-hand side has received a bit of bad publicity in times gone by. Many natural left-handers were forced to write with their right hands, and even the Latin name for left, *sinister*, meant 'dark' and 'evil'. But this is just superstition, and casting a counterclockwise circle to trigger your left side does not have such a purely negative connotation in Magic. It is about subconsciously turning to the direction of the Moon and the night. The counterclockwise circle is cast for going backwards into the past, for cleansing a space or ridding yourself of leftover stress, or working with the deep and the more mysterious witchy energies and your moonshadow side for a change.

The following widdershins, counterclockwise ritual can be used for clearing away negative energies and past worries and for 'washing' a magical space in readiness for further spellcasting and rituals.

Instead of visualizing a sphere of light, imagine you are holding a bowl of water. And as you look into it, start breathing deeply in and out. With each breath, imagine the water is drawing out all your doubts and fears about yourself. As it absorbs those heavy and negative sensations, feel the water revitalize you and recharge you with a sense of inner calm and strength. Whenever you are ready, start spinning to the left, in a counterclockwise direction, flinging the imaginary bowl of water away from you. Watch it flow into a beautiful velvety river of energy that dissolves into the atmosphere, washing over everything with a deep sense of spiritual cleansing and a feeling of release.

CLOSING THE CIRCLE

Some witches like to 'close circle' soon after they have finished casting their Magic and spells. On most occasions I like to retain at least some of the uplifting and energized state of mind, so I simply allow my energies to settle down naturally. I usually spend a few moments in quiet reflection and meditation at the end of each spell or ritual and perhaps say some relaxing words like:

'I now dissolve this circle of power and give thanks to the Universal God/dess'.

Or I may choose to ground myself by sitting comfortably or lying down on either the floor, grass, rock or sand, and feeling the grounding energy gently bringing me back down to earth and everyday reality.

TEMPLE OF THE FOUR WINDS

This magical stone circle was taught to me during my years of apprenticeship with the sorcerer Fenris. It is called the Temple of the Four Winds because it not only honours the power of the four winds but it is also built as a permanent circle of stones, in a similar way to a Druid's temple, and can be entered alone or with guests for meditation, special rituals or spells. If you have enough space outdoors, in your own backyard or terrace, you can build the circle whatever size you like, but if space is a problem, you can build one that is just big enough for one or two people to stand or sit in and then keep it permanently set up as your special outdoor temple.

You will need to gather:

- a wooden stick (this will become your Magic Stang) at least 3 ft (90 cm) long (this can be a slim piece of any tree branch, a broom handle or a simple or ornate walking stick); you will also need to decide which end of the stick you choose to be the top and which is the bottom end
- some chalk or a can of white spray paint (optional)
- a measuring tape (optional)
- a number of pebbles or medium-sized stones (how many depends on how big you decide to make your circle)
- a basket or bag for the stones (optional)
- a cup of sea or rock salt

You can build this stone circle on any reasonably fine morning of the year, but the most powerful time to erect the temple is during summer when the sun is at its strongest peak (particularly the dawn of the Summer Solstice).

If you have already worked out from which direction the Sun rises in your area, then that's all you need to know—where East is. If not, you will need to get a compass to work it out.

The day before you build your temple, look for a safe, quiet spot outside in your back-yard, courtyard, or on an open-air balcony (preferably where you can go and be undis-turbed and relaxed). When you have found the perfect spot, meditate for a while to help cleanse your aura and settle your energies. Then work out the exact position and size you'd like your temple to be (the measuring tape can help here). Next draw a clockwise circle either in the earth with a stick, or with a piece of chalk on the ground, or you can use either a paint brush or can of spray paint. At this point you can also work out if you have enough stones or pebbles to build the temple. Do a test by placing your stones around the traced circle to see if you have enough. The stones don't have to be touching each other; you can place them up to a foot (30 cm) apart if you don't want to collect too many. When you have finished your test and drawn or painted your circle, take away all the stones, and store them outside the circle (in a container or bag if you wish). Then pick up the cup of salt and walk just once around the traced circle in a counterclockwise (widdershins) direction, sprinkling the salt as you go, to cleanse the area. Next, leave the traced circle as it is overnight so the area can be charged by the energy of the Moon.

That night, before you go to sleep, set your alarm clock early so you can be ready to start building at least half an hour before sunrise. In the morning, after you have had a quick wash, you can either dress in some comfortable clothes or remain sky-clad. Then go out and gather all the stones and the wooden stick, go back out into the center of the circle and put the stones and the stick down in the middle. Sit nearby in a comfortable position facing east, and wait for the Sun to rise. As soon as you see the rays of the Sun lighting up the sky, pick up just your wooden stick, stand up, and walk over to the eastern edge of the circle. Hold the stick with the top end pointing majestically up to the sky to be charged by the rays of the morning Sun and say out loud:

> 'Sacred rays of the Eastern Dawn, charge us now with glorious new beginnings and the fire of life.'

Then when you feel ready, walk slowly and evenly around the circle to the right, in a clockwise direction (Deosil) with the stick pointing to the ground in front of you—as if you are retracing the exact line of the circle and now charging it with the Sun's magical energy. Then when you have walked once completely around the circle you should end up back facing the sunrise in the easterly position.

Remain facing the Sun with your arms raised to the sky. Breathe deeply in and out as you feel your lungs being cleansed with fresh air. Hold the stick once more up toward the sky, as you say this incantation with conviction:

'Gather now all four winds of East, North, South and West,
blow from all corners of the Earth, Sun, sky, and sea.
Now together we are as one as we cast this our circle of power.
So Mote it Be.'

Next, walk back into the center of the circle and tap the bottom end of the stick three times on the ground. Then lay the stick down and pick up as many stones as you can (take the container with you if you like) and start placing them one by one in a Deosil (clockwise) direction around the circle. If you need to go back into the center to collect more stones, that's okay; just keep laying them all down in a clockwise direction until you have laid down an evenly spaced circle of stones.

When you have finally finished laying down the stones, go back and stand in the center of your circle. Then pick up the wooden stick once again, turn on the spot and face the sunrise again. Hold the stick for the last time in the sky directly above you as you say:

'I call on the Lords of Light, the goddess Moon and Sun
to honor this our temple of the four winds,
for as long as it stands may this be
a sacred space of Magic and eternal wisdom.
O Blessed Be.'

Finish the ritual by tapping the ground again three times with the bottom end of the stick, and then you may walk out of the temple in any direction. To 'lock up' the energies of the temple while you are away, stand outside it and say:

> 'Between the ways guards the Lords and Goddess of Light,
> we shall go with honor, merry meet, merry part
> and merry meet again.'

Make sure you bring anything left over from the ritual with you and keep your wooden stick in a safe place wrapped in a piece of silk, cotton or leather. Because your stick has been energized by the ritual, it is now called your 'Magic Stang' and it is to be used only by you (or a delegated person) and only when you want to go back and meditate or do some rituals in the temple.

Whenever you wish to reenter the temple for meditation or for special rituals, reopen the magical doorway by standing outside any part of the circle holding your 'Magic Stang'. Tap the bottom end of the stick on the ground three times and say:

> 'I open the ways to greet the blessing of the Lords and
> the Goddess of Light,
> Merry Meet.'

And then walk into the temple.

Once you have opened the magical doorway to the temple, you or any guests can walk in and out from any direction as much as you like. You can bring any spell items or decorations in and out with you and when you have finished your rituals, you or the delegated person are in charge of 'locking' the magical doorway up again with the previous closing ritual.

Don't be surprised if you keep finding your family pet curled up asleep inside it—or if your smallest child always seems to enjoy playing in the middle of this outdoor temple. There's no need to discourage it, as this happens simply because animals and children are naturally attracted to the circle's natural goddess and Fairy vibrations. Their presence is always welcomed and only enhances the magical energies within.

A real witch lives a life filled with free-spirited creativity, a passionate sense of the mystical world, and a boundless love for Earth and Nature

Your Indoor Temple

I like to think of my home as being an indoor temple, with not only rooms for rest, work and sharing food with my friends and family, but also with some special area within where, no matter how deliciously chaotic and untidy the rest of the house may get, I always have my own 'sacred space' for weaving certain spells or to just sit quietly and meditate for a while. My sacred space and magical altar are near a window in my bedroom, where I have placed an old-fashioned dressing table and mirror on which I have strewn all my favorite crystals and seashells and my collection of new and antique perfume bottles. Because I am quite an eclectic witch I am always on the lookout for new and interesting knickknacks, and I also have a variety of candlesticks and magical tools, including a set of pewter chalices and a specially carved bone and crystal wand. Recently I found a small but exquisitely engraved ceremonial knife, which I now use as my 'Athame', and that, along with a plump little statue of the Laughing Buddha, takes pride of place among my collection.

There are lots of different ways to set up your own altar, and while some of the contemporary Craft traditions have very definite rules on which direction you should be facing and what specific tools you should have, I really think that the most enchanting altars are those that contain items you personally treasure, have made yourself, or have chosen because they have called out to you in a shop or a flea market stall and said:

'Try me! I can help you make Magic!'

You can create an altar facing North, in the direction of Dreams and the Moon, or facing East, in the sacred direction of the rising Sun.

What's in a Name?

Magical names can be both inspiring and very useful in creating just the right energy for rituals and spellcasting. The name 'Belthane' is my own adaptation from the witchy festival Beltane, and I love to go by that name during my old coven's favorite celebration, Walpurgisnacht on April 30, and during any of the Spring and Summer rituals, or simply when I feel like adding some extra sunshine and a happy spring feeling into my life.

You don't have to rush out and choose a magical name at all if you don't want to, and funnily enough I have found that a lot of witchy folks I know seem to think that some of the most powerful names actually choose you. For instance, quite a few of my magical friends and I were never Christened or given our birth names through a normal religious ceremony. Instead, each of us went through our first official naming ceremony in very unusual and witchy circumstances. Like many coven-educated witches, I also have a secret Craft name that was given to me in my first-ever naming ceremony, or 'christening' by Fenris the Druidmaster (and I retain its power by keeping it secret and only using it whenever I want to make contact with him). My friend Athena was officially named for the first time in a feather and water ceremony by a Mexican Indian Shaman called Don Juan, who 'christened' her with the name 'Starwoman' in the 1970s. And it has certainly helped to resonate the perfect star essence around her life and work. Athena also tells me that sometimes, when she feels she needs grounding, she calls herself 'Earthwoman' for a few hours—just to have a bit of rest from zooming around the planets. Names definitely resonate around you with their own energy, and each name can inspire you in very different ways.

If you're in search of an enchanting name for your witchy work, then here's a short list of suggested names along with their magical vibrations and meanings.

CELTIC AND GAELIC NAMES
FEMALE

- Aideen: Irish lover of the fairy man
- Aine: fair Queen
- Aislin: dream
- Ashore: loved one
- Brenna: raven maid
- Brigid: strong
- Calum: dove
- Cara: friend
- Darcy: dark one
- Duvessa: dark beauty
- Edana: little fire
- Fenella: fair
- Genevieve: magic sighs
- Gwyneth: white lady
- Keelia: beauty
- Rhiannon/Epona: witch and horse goddess
- Riona: queenly
- Rona: sea
- Sabia: goodness
- Shannon: little wise one
- Ula: jewel of the sea

CELTIC AND GAELIC NAMES
MALE

- Ahern: lord of horses
- Arthur: noble
- Baird: ballad singer
- Bram: raven
- Calhoun: warrior
- Callum: messenger of peace
- Carlin: little champion
- Casey: brave
- Conlan: hero
- Dagda: strong wizard god
- Dallan: wise
- Devin: poet

- Donnovan: dark warrior
- Edan: fiery
- Forbes: wealthy and prosperous
- Galen: intelligent
- Gavin: white hawk
- Hogan: youthful and spirited
- Mahon: bear strength
- Morgan: sea's edge
- Murrough: sea warrior
- Niall: champion energy
- Sheridan: wild man
- Tiernan: lord

GREEK NAMES

FEMALE

- Amarantha: immortal
- Ambrosia: food of life
- Anastasia: one who will rise again
- Astra: starlike
- Calandra: lark and song
- Chloe: flowering
- Delphine: oracle of Apollo
- Dorissa: sea
- Ilona: light
- Iris: goddess of the rainbow
- Melanie: dark beauty
- Moira: goddess of destiny
- Penelope: the weaver
- Phoebe: moon goddess
- Theola: divine
- Trina: pure
- Ursa: she-bear
- Zandra: helper of humankind
- Zoe: life giving

MALE

- Ajax: eagle
- Alexander: great protector
- Cosmo: the world
- Darius: wealthy
- Homer: promise
- Jason: the healer
- Leander: lion man
- Orestes: mountain
- Orion: hunter
- Phalen: calms
- Sebastian: majestic
- Zeno: shining

MISCELLANEOUS CULTURES AND ENERGIES

- Adora: beloved one
- Aurora: golden energy
- Belinda: beautiful serpent
- Bellona: Goddess of War
- Blackthorn: protection
- Bluebird: great name to make you feel happy
- Bryony: balance
- Cerelia: Goddess of the Harvest
- Chantal: singer and enchantress
- Diana: goddess of the hunt
- Draco: dragon lover
- Faline: catlike
- Fayiana: dancer
- Goldenrod: Magical healer
- Hawthorn: an ancient and powerfully witchy name
- Heather: graceful and quietly powerful
- Leandra: lioness and leo aspects
- Lily and Lena: feminine and exotic temptress
- Lucretia: wealthy and clever herbalist

- Lumina: a good name for personal enlightenment
- Luna: Moon Goddess energy
- Lyra: bright star and musically bright
- Mahogany, Orchid and Rowan: great names for exotic looks; gives protection
- Maiea: Goddess of Springtime
- Maris: of the sea
- Portia: offering
- Risa: laughing one

- Sibyl: prophetess and fortune teller
- Terra: Goddess of the Earth
- Valora: strong and courageous

ENCHANTING COMBINATIONS
MALE AND FEMALE

- Aidan Nightwind
- Aldwyn Greenwood
- Annwyn Celestine
- Artemis Dreamweaver
- Astra Angel
- Axel Beowulf
- Axel Ra
- Beowulf Moonstone
- Bram Uther
- Bran Cerridwyn
- Bright Saffron
- Callista Rune Moonstone

- Dagda Avalon
- Danu Morag
- Dru Butterfly
- Druida East Elf
- Earth Serpent Ice
- Edain Maeve Bear
- Edris Arianrhod
- Eldritch Adrian
- Eldritch Osiris
- Eldritch Storm
- Elf-Arrow
- Erlic Danu

- Faery Bringer
- Gaia Rhiannon
- Gandalf Moonshadow
- Gold Cougar
- Gwydion Rain
- Gwyneth Tor
- Ipona Ariel
- Isis Rainbow
- Luna Mist
- Mab Feather Wynn
- Mahogany Wizard Boy
- Merlin Ice Glimmer
- Moonwoman Thunder Hawk
- Morgan Ariadne
- Mystic Silver
- Niamh Acorn

- Raven Moon Crow
- Sky Wolfe
- Star Weaver
- Tara North
- Thunder Angel
- Thunder Lugh Purple
- Western Sky Flame
- Winter Firestorm
- Wolverine Swordbringer

For further reading on this subject, I suggest you pick up a copy of the fantastic book *The Complete Book of Magical Names* by Phoenix McFarland.

Some names, such as 'High Priestess' or 'Elder', are more like titles to describe a level of mastery and years of experience and hold a lot of weight behind them because they are ancient and have deep meanings. While such names are very useful, like any tool they should be used well, with deep respect and, in this case, only where necessary and appropriate.

Be discerning about people you might meet who, after just a year or two of study, call themselves names like 'Most Almighty Powerful One' or 'Grand Highest Pooh-Bah Priestess'. Magical names aren't meant to be used as a form of worship; if they are, sooner or later the effect will wear off.

It's a bit like that great scene in the Disney cartoon *Fantasia* where Mickey Mouse is the Sorcerer's apprentice and starts spinning some broom Magic from the Master's personal spell book. Before long, the spell's power gets away from him and he doesn't have enough knowledge or experience to turn it off again. For us as witches, using a name like 'High Priestess' can be a bit like playing with that Magic from the Master's personal spell book; you could easily be playing out of your depth. Remember, these are ancient terms of mastery, so make sure you are ready for them.

They are powerful and the Magic within them comes with a big responsibility.

104

Ironically, one of the most experienced and clever witches I know, Leonora, who has been quietly practicing the Craft for over 30 years and has lived and taught in a highly respected coven for most of that time, simply likes to call herself a witch or a metaphysic. When I asked her recently why she doesn't use the term 'High Priestess' (and she has certainly earned the right to use it) and rarely dresses in her ceremonial robes during magical workshops, she replied, "Because I want my students to know that they can do this on the bus."

Whatever the case, by all means call yourself any mythical or magical term that inspires and appeals to you, but try not to use a name that weighs you down like an old suitcase, and never lose your sense of humor about yourself.

As my old coven master used to always say, 'When two sorcerers meet, the one who isn't laughing isn't a sorcerer.'

Magic Ways and Means

AROMA MAGIC

Wonderful power springs from the aroma of flowers and plants, and magicians have been practicing and perfecting the mystical art that we now call 'aromatherapy' for thousands of years. Each aromatic plant, fragrant flower, and scented herb has its own essential qualities and scents that can be used in healing massages and baths, in oil burners or in Magic potions and lucky oils.

Many of the commonly used essential oils of aromatherapy are readily available from pharmacies and health food stores, but if you are really keen, you can distill your own floral and herbal essences. But to begin with, you can have lots of fun creating your own enchanted potions with just a few basic essential oils. It might be a good idea to read about the basics of aromatherapy before you begin; there are many books on the subject available in bookshops, new age stores and libraries. You can also simply choose an aroma based on a particular emotion or state of mind from the list of characteristics that follows, or read through the list of Essences for Every Occasion on the following page and pick an oil for its particular properties. The following is an esoteric guide to the use of a magical essence or herb.

AROMA QUICK FINDER

⑥ Love: jasmine, gardenia, rose and neroli

⑥ Lust: basil, cinnamon, ginger, neroli and ylang ylang

⑥ Wealth: bergamot, mint, nutmeg and allspice

⑥ Healing: rosemary, sandalwood and carnation

⑥ Protection: basil, frankincense and lavender

⑥ Money: clove and pine

⑥ Tranquillity: lavender, marjoram, thyme and chamomile

⑥ Uplifting: St John's wort (also good for nervous tension), bay and carnation

⑥ High Magic blessing: benzoin, frankincense and rue

ESSENCES FOR EVERY OCCASION

- ⊚ Eucalyptus: uplifting, cleansing, banishing
- ⊚ Geranium: romance, antidepressant and cleansing
- ⊚ Jasmine: spiritual love, serenity, beauty
- ⊚ Lavender: soothes, heals, calms conflict
- ⊚ Lemon: good fortune and power
- ⊚ Marigold: healing, promotes tranquillity and peace
- ⊚ Mimosa: add to jojoba oil for care of sensitive skin
- ⊚ Mint: joyful, inspirational and energizing
- ⊚ Orange: healing, energy and love
- ⊚ Petitgrain: healing and de-stressing
- ⊚ Rose: love, passion and femininity
- ⊚ Rosemary: sexuality, anxiety and stress
- ⊚ Sandalwood: peace, meditation and cleansing
- ⊚ Ylang ylang: sensuality and happiness

Crystal Power

Precious gems and crystals have been worn both for their beauty and their magical qualities since earliest recorded history. Some gems are known to absorb the warmth and moisture of the skin, and many crystals can change color in different light and atmospheres. Whether you wear them in elaborate necklaces and bracelets or carry a single crystal in your pocket, their powers—mystical and legendary—are equally potent.

BIRTHSTONES

Birthstone Magic can be traced as far back as 4000 BC to the spellcasters of Memphis in Egypt, who wore breastplates encrusted with special gems to protect and empower them with mystical energy.

One of the easiest ways to find your own birthstone is through the help of the stars. Look up your zodiac sign below, and when you have obtained the corresponding crystal, wash it in spring water mixed with a pinch of salt. Dry it well with a clean white cloth and keep it on your desk, altar or in a magical box.

Hold your birthstone on a Full or New Moon in both hands and say:

> 'Stone of power, beautiful giver of light,
> I consecrate you in the name of the
> Triple Goddess of the night.
> And as my will, it shall be right.'

ASTROLOGICAL BIRTHSTONES

- Aries: garnet
- Taurus: turquoise
- Gemini: agate
- Cancer: moonstone
- Leo: amber
- Virgo: carnelian

- Libra: lapis lazuli
- Scorpio: tourmaline
- Sagittarius: topaz
- Capricorn: malechite
- Aquarius: aquamarine
- Pisces: amethyst

Not only are many of these stones bright and alluring, but each also has its own special and enchanted attributes. To use a gem in a spell, choose whatever charm you would like to cast and wash the appropriate crystal in some spring water mixed with a pinch of rosemary. Dry the crystal well with a clean, white cloth, and leave it near a window for a day and a night to be charged by the power of both the Sun and the Moon.

The following list outlines the properties of gems often used as charms and in spells.

CRYSTALS AND THEIR PROPERTIES

- ◎ Amethyst: for courage, emotional love, success
- ◎ Aventurine: attracts calming energy, luck, intelligence, clear eyesight and money
- ◎ Azurite: helps psychic powers, dreams and meditation
- ◎ Carnelian: dispels jealousy and anger, develops sexuality
- ◎ Citrine: for psychic awareness and creativity, dispels nightmares
- ◎ Haematite: for grounding, divination and intuition
- ◎ Jasper: for health, beauty and protection
- ◎ Lapis Lazuli: promotes healing, love, fidelity and psychic powers
- ◎ Moonstone: for divination, youth and Moon Magic
- ◎ Onyx: for protection and defensive Magic, helps control passions and emotions
- ◎ Tiger's-eye or Cat's-eye: attracts courage, luck and Earth energy
- ◎ Turquoise: attracts money, love, friends and healing
- ◎ Clear Quartz: magnifies psychic and healing energy; a power and protection crystal
- ◎ Smoky Quartz: overcomes depression and fatigue; empowering

Magic Moments, Seasons and Times

Connecting with the universal source of Magic has no time limits. It can be done at any second of the day and in any week of the year with great results, but there are certain Moon phases, seasons and witching hours that can give an extra boost to your spellcasting and can help bring longer-lasting effects.

MOON POWER

One of the most popular of the tried and true methods is to align a particular type of spell or ritual with the corresponding phase of the Moon. Even the most sceptical scientists know that the Moon directly effects not only the Earth's tides, but also our most basic animal and human emotions. Many people are sensitive to the Moon's changing phases, and all women of childbearing age are both physically and emotionally affected through their own natural and 'lunar'-based monthly cycles. Most witches keep a current Moon calendar handy (they can be purchased at New Age stores, or you can also look for a fishing guide in your local newsstand) so they can cast a close eye on the changing lunar cycles. The Moon orbits the Earth in a counterclockwise (widdershins) direction and has an approximate 28-day cycle as it grows, or waxes from the first day of the New Moon up to the Full Moon. It then goes into a diminishing, or waning, phase back to begin the cycle all over again. Each of these different phases has a corresponding effect on your ritual.

> ◎ Full Moon: for casting spells of love and high Magic
> ◎ New Moon: to begin a new relationship or job
> ◎ Waxing or Growing Moon: to attract growth, prosperity and commitment
> ◎ Waning or Diminishing Moon: to finish a relationship or to banish negative energy

LUNAR CYCLES

There are 13 Full Moons (Esbats) in the year, and a Full Moon is a very powerful time for spellcasting and rituals.

The Harvest Moon is the Full Moon nearest the Autumn Equinox (Mabon).

'Once in a Blue Moon' happens in a year when a Full Moon appears twice in the same month.

DAYS OF ENCHANTMENT

Another clever aid to spellcasting is to align your ritual with the corresponding day of the week. This can be very handy as a stopgap alignment where perhaps you want to cast a love spell or a prosperity charm, but, due to time constraints, can't wait for a new or Full Moon to give it a mystical kick in the right direction. Each day of the week is ruled by at least one corresponding planet, so each particular day picks up the heavenly aspects of its very own guiding star.

◎ Sunday: Sun energy for casting spells of healing and tranquillity, and to invoke divine power

◎ Monday: Moon energy for beginnings, employment, clairvoyance and family

◎ Tuesday: Mars energy for debates, courage, physical strength and lust

◎ Wednesday: Mercury's influence for learning, teaching, predictions, self-improvement and communication

◎ Thursday: Jupiter power for wealth, legal matters, luck, materialism and expansion

◎ Friday: Venus energy for love, pleasure, art, music and partnerships

◎ Saturday: Saturn's influence for finalization, departure and resolution

Sun Worship

Most people automatically associate the Moon and the stars with the old craft of Magic, but the Sun is also an ancient and constant symbol of wonder and enchantment, and many of the sacred sites around the world were dedicated to either the Sun God or Goddess. Sunrise and midday are both perfect times to celebrate the precious life-giving solar rays, and performing rituals at either time of the day can greatly enhance the power of certain spells.

Dawn Sun

The 'new born' sunrays at dawn have been revered since ancient times because the sunrise has always been considered sacred and an eternal miracle to behold. Sunrise can be a great time to enhance outdoor rituals or any kind of spells which incorporate new beginnings, abundance and fertility and power. The dawn of Midsummer Solstice is still considered the most powerful time of all, but for a modern witch any sunrise is just as awe inspiring and miraculous and can be used to empower many ceremonies and spellworking.

MIDDAY SUN

As the Sun is at its peak it is another peak time for Magic, and this hour has a double solar whammy because it's directly opposite to the Moon-flavored midnight and is backed up by the Magical power of the number 12.

My favorite spells to cast at midday are those that need a really big boost of life force, such as spells for getting over heartache and grief and also spells for prosperity and business dealings.

You can also dedicate a simple indoor or outdoor altar to the Sun by decorating a table with summertime flowers—especially sunflowers or yellow blooms—as well as seashells, aromatic potpourri and oranges and lemons.

Special colors associated with the Sun include white, red, corn yellow, and of course gold. Ritual candles can also include the color blue to represent the sky in combination with yellow, red or gold.

The best crystals for Sun rituals include all green gemstones, especially emerald and jade as well as amber and yellow gems such as sapphires. Other powerful gemstones are tiger's-eye and lapis lazuli. Spells should include the incenses of frankincense, sandalwood and ylang ylang, and for extra enchantment add the essential oils of saffron, lavender or clove to your oil burner. If you have your own herb garden, herbs gathered during the dawn or midday (particularly during midsummer) are extremely powerful and can be dried to use during the rest of the year.

To stimulate your creative ideas and imagination, create your own fantasy spells with pictures of enchanted animals associated with the Sun. Some favorites are sparrows and canaries, and mythical creatures like unicorns, firebirds, dragons and satyrs.

Leave a small mirror near your window for seven days to capture the light of the Sun. On the eighth day, sprinkle it with spring water and recite this self-dedication spell to attract success and happiness:

> 'O Goddess, I see you gaze through golden eyes;
> so silently you speak your words.
> A delicate stroll through crystal sands,
> curling through perfumed corridors.
> Now let this ancient alchemy awaken you,
> let your sacred light come to me at last.'

ENCHANTED SEASONS

The changing seasons bring different energies, and we can perform ceremonies to help align us with the ebb and flow, the light and dark aspects of the natural universe and also to empower our spellworking. There are both contemporary rituals and old folklore ways to celebrate the seasons, and for many witches, the magical Wheel of the Year influences not only our physical and spiritual connections to these cycles of climatic change, but also the eternal shape-shifting and merging of God and Goddess energies within nature and ourselves.

Symbolically, as the Wheel of the Year turns, the Great Mother Goddess gives birth to the Sun 'child' at Yule, and as the magical Wheel keeps turning, the Triple Moon Goddess helps to purify the newborn energies and light up the night of Imbolc. Spring Equinox sees the developing of the young Sun God, who is promised in marriage to the budding Maiden Goddess. As Beltane and Summer arrive and the Sun God fully matures into his physical form, he then appears on Earth as the powerful King Stag and makes passionate love to his fertile Goddess bride, the Queen Fairy of the Flowers.

At Lugnasad comes the symbolic cutting of the mystical chord by the scythe of the Dark Sky Goddess, which also marks the last days of the Sun God's life in the earthly physical realm.

Then as the Autumn Equinox passes and the Old 'Hag' Goddess returns to cover the Earth in her Winter robe of ice and snow, the Sun God travels down into the realm of the spirits and underworld, where he becomes the Lord of the Hallows—only to be reborn as the Sun Child again at Yule through the nurturing belly, the eternal Magic cauldron of the Mother Goddess.

In the ancient pagan countryside, important fertility rites were performed during festival days to help balance the Earth's natural forces or to keep the gods contented and happy. Even in today's urbanized world, many neopagans and witches follow as much as they can of the old ways.

The following festivals (also known as the Major Sabbats) date way back in time to the days of the ancient Celts, when Druid priests and priestesses were in charge of most religious and magical ceremonies.

◎ Samhain: One of the most ancient and biggest Celtic festivals marking the beginning of the old Druid year (which was originally based on a lunar calendar). A deeply spiritual and nocturnal time for long nights of hibernation and communing with the ancestors. Festivities often lasted the whole month of November.

◎ Imbolc: Post-Winter festival of the ancient Celts with purification ceremonies to reveal the first rays of sacred light and the blessing of the triple goddess, Brigid.

◎ Beltane: The other major festival for the Celts, the full re-awakening of the Earth and the return of daylight and the Sun god Bel. The virility of the natural world and the regenerating power of light were celebrated with bonfires and fertility and flower rites.

◎ Lugnasad: Honouring Lugh (the great warrior god of skills and knowledge) and the Mother Goddess (symbol of Ireland). A royal festival led by Lugh's earthly counterpart, the Celtic King, and celebrated with horse racing, dancing and poetry competitions.

Most other old Europeans, particularly the Germanic and Nordic people, enjoyed very similar kinds of festivals around the same days, but they also set aside extra days and rituals to mark the Winter and Summer Solstice as well as the Autumn and Spring Equinox. Throughout the ages and after constant invasions of the British Isles and Europe, there have been lots of mixing and blending between the Celtic, Gaelic and Germanic magical traditions and these four additional festivals (also called Minor Sabbats) are also celebrated by today's Wiccans as well as many other witches and neopagans.

⑥ Mabon: Autumn Equinox   ⑥ Yule: Midwinter Solstice
⑥ Ostara: Spring Equinox   ⑥ Litha: Midsummer Solstice

121

WHEEL OF THE YEAR

Not all covens or solitary witches perform rituals on all eight sabbats (or during all 13 esbats, and full moons) and there's no need to feel as if you must slavishly follow every single custom and festival. The Craft is constantly evolving and adaptations are always being made—particularly by city witches or by those who live in areas of the world where the seasonal changes are different or not so well defined. Whatever days you set aside for spiritual rituals or celebration should be your own choice and will depend very much on what kind of traditions you or your magical group relate to—and of course, what you can personally fit in with your own family commitments and work schedule. Any of these sabbats and festival days can also be honored beautifully and simply by having a celebratory meal with a few family members and friends, or just by lighting a candle and giving yourself a quiet moment alone for spiritual reflection and energy alignment.

Following is a list of festival days that has been clarified for modern living, plus some tips on how these days can also be used to enhance both your meditation rituals and spellworking.

◎ Lugnasad (Lammas)

AUGUST 1

This was traditionally around the time of harvest, to celebrate the various skills and talents of the people. For us modern witches, it can be a time for emotional 'harvesting' as we take stock of our lives and remember not to take our own talents for granted—nor the blessings and abundance of the Earth. Take the time to really look on the bright side of life and spend some quality hours outdoors enjoying nature as much as you can, before the Autumn weather starts to set in. It is also a good time for defining what your talents are, writing down mission statements and casting prosperity spells.

◎ Mabon

APPROX. SEPTEMBER 20-22 (AUTUMN EQUINOX)

This is a perfect time to start a saving program so that you can see what you can afford to put aside and store for the long Winter months ahead. Start being more careful not to waste time and being more discerning about what projects and problems to take on. The best rituals at this time are ones for creating balance and counting blessings. The night and day are of equal length, and this is a time of natural equilibrium, so you may use it to meditate and hone your visionary skills.

⊚ Samhain (Halloween)

OCTOBER 31

Many witches around the world celebrate their own magical New Year's Eve on this ancient night of 'All Hallows Eve'. This deeply spiritual and significant evening marks the symbolic passing over into the mystical 'shadow' world. The hidden veil between the spiritual realm and the 'real' world is now at it's thinnest—it's party time at the edge of 'hedge' of reality, so naturally—it can be a—superbly witchy time for communing with Guardian Angels or ancestral spirits, as well as casting banishing spells or dispelling negative and unwanted vibrations from your home and workplace.

⊚ Yule

APPROX. DECEMBER 20-22 (MIDWINTER SOLSTICE)

In ancient pagan times they celebrated the rebirth of the 'Sun Child' or 'Holly King' during Yule, and it is said that many of the old familiar Yule traditions were adapted by later churches and added into the popular Christmas celebrations. Whatever religious traditions or spiritual path you follow you can also utilize this time to empower yourself with the ancient ways and the energy of rebirth and growth. This is the shortest day of the year, where the Earth and the Sun appear to be stilled and suspended together for a moment in time, so this a very magical day and evening for rituals that can align you with the timeless aspects of the eternal Universe. Spellworking can be enhanced by communing with both your inner child and nurturing Mother Goddess energies.

⊚ Imbolc (or Candelmas)
FEBRUARY 2

A great time for candle Magic for purification and celebrating the Moon. Also great for witchy initiations or reaffirming partnership vows. The Celtic traditions celebrated Brigid the Triple Goddess so you can also weave spells and rituals that incorporate Brigid or any of the Luna Goddess energies. Generally a good time for bringing some light into the shadowy or darker areas of your life and 'lightening up' by looking at the funny side of things, as well as pampering yourself with long baths or relaxing massages. Excellent too for house cleansing and banishing rituals with the sweeping of brooms both clockwise and anticlockwise.

⊚ Ostara

APPROX. MARCH 20-22 (SPRING EQUINOX)

The light and dark energies are in perfect balance, and this is the dawning of the major solar festivals. The youthful Sun god and Maiden goddess energies are flowing through the Earth and rituals are best performed at daytime to take advantage of new possibilities, budding relationships and exciting projects. As well as reconnecting with the bloom of youthful vitality, perform any rituals that can help put a spring in your step and take full advantage of the potent vibrations around you.

⊚ Beltane and May Day

APRIL 30 AND MAY 1ST

Lusty and joyous times with all the family and Magical friends coming together in a full celebration of the love of life as well as the blessing of procreation and fertility. Both days are great for marriage and handfasting rituals or baby naming ceremonies, also excellent times for candle Magic, casting luck and Fairy spells, along with boosting either physical or spiritual fertility with abundance rituals and potent sex Magic.

In Germany April 30th is also 'Walpurgisnacht', a powerful and legendary night when all the witches of the world mystically come together and dance around the fabled Brocken mountain (This night was and still is my coven's most important celebration and always proved to be a special and sacred evening with my teacher Fenris and our inner circle).

⊚ Litha
APPROX. JUNE 20-22 (MIDSUMMER SOLSTICE)

The longest day of the year, traditionally a powerful time for solar rituals and honoring the peak strength of the solar life force. Many ancient temples and sacred sites were built with special altars and archways that captured the Sun's Magical rays during the Summer Solstice and this is a great time of the year to capture some of this miraculous energy for yourself. Great for spells of empowerment, growth and all forms of energizing Magic.

127

essential witchery

spells, rituals and practical Magic

Part Three

Get in Touch With the Witch Within: Rites of Awakening

EARTHING YOURSELF

This ritual involving a tree can be used to align yourself with Earth—to feel grounded and to create the energy of that element in your life and spells, and to connect with the Magic of Earth itself.

You will need to gather:

⑥ *A long length of string (to be removed from tree after ritual)*

Wrap and tie the string around the trunk of a large tree. Give it a big hug, then sit down on the ground with your back and spine aligned against the trunk and become conscious of the solidness of the ground beneath you. When you begin to feel yourself being pulled downward and gaining strength and a solid foundation to your mind and body, repeat this incantation:

'Great Mother Earth, hold me in your arms of green and bring me close to your body of warmest brown. I join with the strength and rhythm of your deepest eternal heart. So Mote It Be.'

HIGH AS A KITE

Take advantage of lovely breezes and windy weather to align with the magical element of Air.

You will need to gather:

⊚ *a length of blue material or ribbon*

On a breezy day, tie one end of the fabric or ribbon to a fence, a tree branch or a clothesline. Then, stand and watch the ribbon fly and wave in the wind. While consciously feeling the breeze, say these words out loud:

'Now blow you winds from North and South,
warm then cold from East to West,
spin and turn, fly and flow,
whisper charms wherefore you go.'

Leave the ribbon in place for as long as you like. You can also add more for family and friends to enjoy.

BECOME ONE WITH WATER

Sit near a lake, swim in the ocean or walk in a light rain as a first step to working with the magical natural element of Water.

Then call on Manannan mac Lir, a sea god and, in the old Celtic world, a Master of Magic. He is also known as the 'Lord of Mists' and 'Lord of the Land Beneath the Waves'. Think of his strength and call his name when you want to invoke a strong sense of the ocean and the mystical seas.

'Hail to you Manannan mac Lir, Lord of the Mists, Lord of the Waves—
I feel your strength from between the Ways,
In the eye of the storm, your heart beats like a drum
From the salty depths of the Sea we rise up now—together as one!'

FEEL THE FIRE

Element of Fire

Whenever you are lucky enough to sit by an open fire really take the time to absorb the energy, breathe in the wonderful smell of the burning wood and think about what an amazing gift it is. For an easy connection with the element of fire, simply light a candle and sit nearby while gazing at the center of the flame. Without coming too close or blowing out the flame, wave your hand near the candle and feel the warmth and observe how the flame moves and dances around. Then just sit quietly a short distance away and really focus your mind on the flame and see whether you can 'will' the candle flame to move up and down or right and left or spin around just by thinking about it. To help you focus on this part of the ritual, say this incantation a few times:

> 'Sacred flame, do as I say,
> Sacred flame, dance and play.'

When you feel energized and ready to end the ritual, say these words:

> 'Sacred flame, do as I will,
> Sacred flame, now be still.'

And then blow out the flame completely.

COSMIC AWAKENER AND SELF-INITIATION

Two of the most treasured and valuable lessons I've learned through my own journey is that we are all connected to the eternal source of Magic and that every spiritual path in the world holds symbolic keys to cosmic truth and meaning. We are all part of an ancient Universal Tradition.

This ritual helps awaken you to the boundless source of cosmic knowledge and can also be used as a self-initiation into Universal Magic.

Spend time meditating on each of the symbols written below; you can even copy or trace them out on a piece of paper if you wish. Focus for at least seven minutes on each symbol until you've concentrated on all of them, and do this once a day, in either the morning or the evening, for no less than 21 days.

Symbols are the Celtic cross, the ankh, the star of David, the yin and yang symbol, the witch's star pentacle, the eye of Horus, the infinity symbol and the spiral.

After you have performed this 21-day ritual, look into a mirror and say:

*'I am a magical and eternal being
of the Universe and I awaken the witch within.'*

PAST-LIFE VISION BOOSTER

To help you get a clearer view of past lives, cast this spell on the day of a New Moon and repeat it once every week for a month.

Take a small white onion and soak it in a bowl of mineral water for half an hour and then take it out and dry it thoroughly with a clean cloth. Meditate for a few minutes while you hold the onion in your hands and then start to peel off the first and second layers of the onion while you repeat this incantation:

'Memories of the distant past, come forward into the light.'

Place the layers you have peeled off into a paper bag and bury near a tree. Keep the rest of the onion wrapped in the refrigerator to use again.

Don't just believe it can happen, know it and see that it already has.

God and Goddess Power

Lift the veil of superstition when you talk to the gods and goddesses. Losing yourself to fear or superstition is magically disempowering. We can still commune and feel at one with all the inspirational magic of the ancient gods and goddesses without bowing down or feeling less worthy than they are.

There's also no need to look at the god/dess energies as if they are completely separate from you, because that is a psychological giving up of your personal power.

Knowing you are responsible for your own thoughts and actions is magically empowering. A real witch is a lead player in her own game of life.

You are just as much a part of the cosmic order as are the god and goddess energies. Summoning the ancient gods and goddesses is a summoning up of the natural forces and the different personas within yourself, which helps connect you with the myriad of archetypal energies throughout the universe.

As my good friend and sister witch Leonora says: 'There is quite a difference between praying to a great goddess and just saying "please help me", and saying, "Dear Great Goddess, I am you and you are me".

'Saying it without arrogance and knowing that you not only communicate with and are a part of the gods, you *are* the goddess and gods, you *are* the rain, you *are* the earth, the sky, you are that big, that all-knowing.

'And even if that realization, that knowing, is just for a split second during ritual or while simply meditating and connecting to your Magic, that's okay, because that is true Magic—knowing you are All That Is.'

I've chosen some of my favorite god/dess spells to remind you that every one of us can be empowered by our inner Magic. With the right incantation, you can also call on whatever type of god/dess nature you need to inspire and balance your life.

THE WARRIOR

When you need to use your warrior energy and assertive nature (this can be a god or goddess ritual), rise early on a Monday morning and cast this spell before you begin your daily routine.

Take a refreshing shower using an aloe body gel and a firm sponge or loofah to slough off any dull and dry skin from your body.

Stand under the warm water while you wash away all of your timid energy and shyness. Feel yourself being filled with new vigor and energy.

When you feel refreshed, wrap yourself in a large towel and look into your bathroom mirror as you say:

> *'I am the Warrior, I recognize my eternal strength.*
> *There's nothing I cannot achieve, no road I cannot travel,*
> *no barriers to my success.*
> *I am woman (man) full of power.'*

YOUNG GOD/DESS

Recognize and have fun with your inner child by casting this spell at any time you need an energy lift.

You will need to gather:

- ◎ gold glitter
- ◎ glue
- ◎ a pair of your old shoes

Place all your spell ingredients on a flat surface and coat the outside of your shoes with glue.

Sprinkle the gold glitter evenly over the gluey shoes, covering as much of the surface area you can. Leave to dry completely.

When the shoes are dry to touch, stand in front of a full-length mirror in your home and slip into the shoes. Then click your heels together three times, look into the mirror and say:

> 'Hello again, young child, let's come out to play.
> We'll have fun and joy forever more
> and inside me you'll always stay.'

Put on your Magic shoes whenever you need a boost of happiness.

THE NURTURING GOD/DESS

All women (and men) can enjoy their independent natures and at the same time still connect with their nurturing and maternal instincts. To honor your inner Earth Mother energy, cast this spell on a Sunday afternoon.

You will need to gather:

- ⑥ an egg
- ⑥ a piece of whole wheat bread
- ⑥ a trowel or spade

Go outside to a safe place in either your backyard or a park and sit down on the ground with your spell items around you.

Hold the egg and bread in your hands while you breathe deeply and focus on your gentle and maternal nature. Then say:

'From Mother Nature we are all born,
nurturing, protective and giver of life.
I now connect with my nurture energy, O Blessed Be.'

Next, dig a hole in the ground and bury the egg and bread in the earth.

THE MYSTIC GOD/DESS

We often forget to look after our spiritual and psychic nature, and this spell can help align you with the cosmic energies around you.

You will need to gather:

- ⊚ a clear quartz crystal
- ⊚ red henna powder or nontoxic red water-based paint
- ⊚ a small paintbrush

Find some time to be alone and undisturbed for at least half an hour, and dress in some comfortable, light-colored clothing.

Using the paintbrush, apply a small red dot to your third eye chakra (on your forehead) and also paint a dot on the palm of each of your hands.

Sit cross-legged on the floor while you hold the crystal in your two hands and breathe calmly and deeply while you meditate and let go of thoughts of daily stresses and worries.

Next, repeat this incantation:

'Thank you, oh universe,
for my awareness of the eternal power of spirit.
I open my psychic mind to the Mystic God/dess.'

THE WISE WO/MAN

Our experiences and ups and downs in life make us wiser and more able to make tough decisions. To help honor our growing maturity and wisdom, cast this spell on any day of the week.

You will need to gather:

- 1 cup of salt
- a handful of cloves

Go to a quiet place in your home.

Stand in the center of the room and sprinkle the salt in a clockwise circle around you.

Then sprinkle the cloves in a clockwise direction around you. Stand in the middle of this circle, with your arms in the air, as you repeat this incantation:

> 'Spirit of the North, grant me knowledge and tolerance,
> blessed be the wo/man within me
> who brings wisdom and understanding.'

Seal the spell's power by scooping up the salt and cloves from the floor and keep the mixture in a small wooden or cardboard box.

143

Ye Olde Apothecary

SETTING UP YOUR ENCHANTED KITCHEN

In centuries past, both the country and town folk would ask their village 'witch doctor' to cook them up a healing brew in times of illness, or a potion to fire up their fertility or chances for romance. These old wise people were really the original medicos. Going back as far in history as ancient Europe, Asia and Egypt (and let's not forget the African and Australian continents), they understood the healing power of herbs and insect and animal products. Certain cultures used a specially brewed beer (an original form of tetracycline), moldy bread (penicillin), snake, toad and spider venoms (antidisease and anticancer properties).

Along with being clever herbalists, many of these witchy medicos were also adept clairvoyants and psychics. They spent many of their days (and, of course, nights) brewing up spellbinding goodies over their bubbling cauldrons and enchanted kitchen fires.

You'll most probably want to skip the snake and wiggly spider bits (handling disagreeable toads is a favorite pastime of mine, but that's another story). There's plenty of scope for you to brew up delicious and magically healing recipes, using safe and palatable ingredients.

I like to write my recipes either in a computer file or an old school exercise book that I've had for years and I still call both systems 'Ye Olde Cookery Book'.

You don't have to go overboard with your 'enchanted kitchen'. If space is a problem, you can make one like mine, which is really about making a specific area in a kitchen or cupboard where you can store your witchy ingredients. As long as they're properly tagged, you can store herbs and things in well-washed coffee or jam jars on your kitchen counter. You could also have a lot of fun with it and make a really 'witchy feature' in your kitchen where you can hang a straw broom and pretty dried flowers, and grow fresh herbs in small pots.

MAGIC KITCHEN BASICS

When you first begin to create your own spells and rituals, you might like to put together your own basic spell kit. This could include:

⊚ A mortar and pestle (preferably stone or metal) for grinding and mixing herbs and spices.

- A variety of glass containers, such as well-washed coffee or jam jars, for storing ingredients and potions.
- A small metal tea-ball for brewing single cups of herbal teas and tonics.
- Pieces of cheesecloth, which are useful for straining brews and for making sachets.
- A tea kettle and a china or metal teapot for magical infusions.
- A cauldron is optional; you can still stir up beautiful Magic with a selection of modern pots and pans.

INGREDIENTS AND SAUCERY—ALMONDS

- **Esoteric Magic**—has an erotic and arousing vibration and is also used in love and fertility spells.
- **Practical Magic**—healing and beauty treatments. Famed for their beautiful flavor and wonderful healing powers in ancient Greece and Rome, the oil, meal and milk of almonds were used in tonics, breads and skin creams well before Christian times.

Hands of Aphrodite

For smooth and blemish-free hands and arms, mix together this ancient recipe on either a Friday (the day of Venus or Aphrodite) or during a waning, diminishing moon.

You will need to gather:

- 3/4 cup of raisins or sultanas
- 3/4 cup of blanched almonds (unsalted and peeled)
- 1 teaspoon of lemon juice
- half a cup of full cream milk (not skim)
- approx half a cup of flat beer (any type will do)

First put the raisins and the blanched almonds into your mortar dish and grind them with your pestle (you can use an electric blender if you prefer). Then add the lemon juice and slowly add the milk. Mix well with a wooden spoon. Next, drip in the beer a little bit at a time, just enough until you have a nice, thick paste.

Then before you take your next shower or bath, wipe the mixture over the back of your hands and over your arms (you can even put it over your entire body if you wish) and leave it on for at least 15 minutes, and then wash it off thoroughly in your shower.

Throw away the remaining mixture and just make a fresh batch the next time you give yourself the 'Aphrodite' treatment.

ALOE VERA

- **Esoteric Magic**—has a peaceful and cleansing vibration, and can be used in protection and healing spells.

- **Practical Magic**—an essential healing plant for just about everything. Every witch should have an aloe vera plant growing in a pot or her garden, and they are very easy to maintain indoors or outdoors. It also soothes sunburned skin and heals scars.

Vera Vitality

This healing drink is best freshly made in the morning and drunk before you get on with the day's activities. It helps cleanse the kidneys and liver, and will give you extra vitality.

You will need to gather:

- *aloe vera gel (break off a small piece of your aloe vera plant and scoop out the inside gel with a spoon—don't eat the skin)*
- *some of your favorite fruit or vegetable juice*

Before you eat your breakfast, pour out a small or medium glass of juice. Squeeze in the aloe vera gel and stir briskly with a long spoon and drink at your leisure.

APPLES

- **Esoteric Magic**—the magic symbol for love and fertility. The emblem of Aphrodite or Venus. One of the sacred Druid trees.

- **Practical Magic**—an apple a day keeps the doctor away, as well as being a natural teeth cleaner. Apple juice is a blood cleanser and is packed full of vitamins.

Apple Water

This old recipe is for a healing drink for fevers and hot flushes.

You will need to gather:

- 3–4 apples, unpeeled
- I quart (I litre) of water
- a teaspoon of sugar

Slice the apples thinly, cover with the water in a saucepan, add the sugar and simmer until the apple slices become soft.

Strain the liquid and allow to cool to room temperature. Throw away the apple slices and drink the liquid either warm or ice cold.

BLACKBERRIES

⟲ **Esoteric Magic**—robust and lively vibrations used for both health and romantic spells and potions.

⟲ **Practical Magic**—a favorite of the ancient Europeans; both the fruit and juice were used for medicinal purposes.

Blackberry Booster

Blackberries have been used for centuries by spellcasters to energize the body. You can use this recipe to make a healing drink or an external compress (see below).

You will need to gather:

⟲ *1 cup of fresh blackberries*
⟲ *1–2 tablespoons of sugar or honey*
⟲ *mineral or spring water (or brandy)*
⟲ *a few cloves*
⟲ *a glass jar with a lid*

Press the juice out of the blackberries, and add the cloves and sugar or honey. Heat in a saucepan and simmer until the mixture becomes syrupy. Allow it to cool and store in the glass jar.

To make a refreshing magical drink, add a spoonful to a glass of mineral or spring water, or heat some syrup and drink it warm with a nip of brandy.

CHAMOMILE

- **Esoteric Magic**—chamomile's vibrations are peaceful and curative, and it is used for meditative and healing spells.

- **Practical Magic**—an ancient remedy for nausea and mental stress. One of the nine sacred herbs of the Saxons, who called it 'maythen', chamomile can also be grown near sick plants to improve their health. It can be drunk as a tea, and also can be used in skin care products and hair care.

CORIANDER

- **Esoteric Magic**—increases hypnotic vibrations and is used for tranquillity and psychic spells.

- **Practical Magic**—pieces of coriander seed were found carefully wrapped in the tomb of the Egyptian Pharaoh Rameses. Used for thousands of years in medicine and for magical foods and sauces.

GARLIC

- **Esoteric Magic**—protective and purifying resonance; its vibrations are steeped in occult history. Necklaces can be made from stringing together fresh or dried bulbs and hung up around the kitchen for good luck. It can also be used for banishing and protective spells.

- **Practical Magic**—highly esteemed by both old and new witchy doctors and used for thousands of years as a food and medicine. One of the first known antibacterial agents since ancient times. Eases sore throats, colds and flu and helps to lower high blood pressure and cholesterol levels. The fresh garlic bulb contains the best healing properties and is much better than the tablets.

Kickagermjoy Juice

Try this amazing healing potion for cleansing the liver and blood. It is especially good for helping to clear up a bad flu and also chest colds.

- *3 or 4 whole garlic bulbs*
- *honey to taste*
- *1 ginger root*
- *5 lemons*
- *8 cups of water*

Peel and roughly chop up all of the garlic bulbs and put them into a large saucepan. Pour in the eight glasses of water.

Chop up the lemons and ginger and also put into the saucepan.

Bring the water to a boil and simmer on low for 5 minutes. Turn off the heat and let it sit for another 10 minutes, then strain off the liquid into another saucepan or a jug and throw away the leftover solids. Drink a cup of the liquid with honey for taste and keep the rest in the refrigerator for up to two days and reheat when needed. (You can add more water if it tastes too strong for you.)

GINGER

- **Esoteric Magic**—uplifting and passionate vibrations for prosperity and love potions
- **Practical Magic**—used for thousands of years in Asian medicine. Antibacterial and good for colds and clearing sinuses, and to relieve mild constipation. Adds zip and zing to any dish, especially fish and chicken dishes.

Magic is real and dreams can come true.

GOAT'S MILK AND YOGURT

◉ **Esoteric Magic**—cleansing and beautifying resonance, used in love and sex potions and beauty spells.

◉ **Practical Magic**—the original glamour queens of Babylon and ancient Egypt swore by the beautifying power of goat's milk, and interestingly enough, it has now been scientifically proven to contain alpha-hydroxy agents as well as the best kind of healing bacteria. Cleo and the rest of the ancient Divas drank and bathed in goat's milk products, and so should any 'glamour-savvy' witch.

Pour half a bottle of goat's milk into your bath along with a dash of lavender for soft, healthy skin; mix the other half of the bottle with some fresh strawberries or bananas for a power-packed breakfast drink.

HONEY

◉ **Esoteric Magic**—resonance of passion and love, used in witchery for fertility, romance and marriage spells.

◉ **Practical Magic**—a fantastic all-around health food and source of vitamins. Used in ancient Europe and Egypt in food and drink and to soothe burns and dry skin.

Honey and Roses

You will need to gather:

- ⑥ a tub of natural honey
- ⑥ 1 cup of fresh rose petals (any color, but red is the strongest) from roses that have been grown without pesticides
- ⑥ 3 cups of water

Boil the rose petals in the water. Simmer for five minutes and then turn off the heat and leave to stand for 10 minutes. Strain the rose water into a jug, and throw away the petals. Mix the honey into the rose water and store in an airtight container in the refrigerator, where it will keep for at least a month or so. It can be used for sore throats or mouth ulcers by simply adding a few teaspoons of the honey rose mixture to herbal tea as a healthy and enchanting drink.

HORSERADISH

- ⑥ **Esoteric Magic**—strong protective vibrations and cleansing resonance. Used for banishing spells.
- ⑥ **Practical Magic**—since olden times, used as a remedy for digestive problems. It was also wrapped into warm cloths and put around limbs and joints to relieve mild rheumatism.

Remedial Recipe

You will need to gather:

- ⊚ 1 teaspoon of horseradish
- ⊚ 1 teaspoon of dry, mild mustard (French mustard is good)
- ⊚ 1 cup of apple-cider vinegar
- ⊚ 2 cups of water
- ⊚ 3 long pieces of cheesecloth

Mix the horseradish, mustard, vinegar and water together in a saucepan. Heat the mixture on the stove for 5 minutes.

Next, turn off the heat and allow the mixture to stand until it reaches room temperature. Then dip in one of the lengths of cheesecloth and wrap it around your aching joint (make sure there are no scratches or open wounds around the joint or it could sting a bit).

Then follow with the next two layers of dry cheesecloth and leave on for at least 20 minutes.

LEMONS AND LIMES

⑥ **Esoteric Magic**—uplifting and cleansing vibration, to enhance renewal. Used in energizing spells and banishing rituals.

⑥ **Practical Magic**—relieves colds, sore throats and fever, warts, insect bites and greasy skin. A fantastic source of vitamin C and used in many magical foods and healing drinks.

Lemon Lift

Make this delicious and uplifting tea, which helps reduce fever, during flu or chest colds.

You will need to gather:

⑥ 1 lemon or 2 limes
⑥ 1 teaspoon of honey (optional)
⑥ 1 cup of hot water
⑥ 1 teaspoon of raspberry jam
⑥ 1 or 2 fresh mint leaves (optional)

Squeeze the lemon or limes, and pour the juice into the bottom of a cup. Stir in the jam and honey (to taste), then pour in the hot water to fill the rest of the cup. Add the mint leaves if you wish and then drink at any time of the day or especially before bed if you have a cold.

LEMON BALM

- **Esoteric Magic**—soothing and calming vibrations. Used for family and home protection spells.

- **Practical Magic**—has been used for many centuries as a wound dressing. It also makes a nice-tasting and mildly sedative tea to help you sleep. You can purchase tea bags or loose tea and pour on hot water with honey or raw sugar for taste before bedtime for a restful night's sleep.

MINT

- **Esoteric Magic**—activating and clearing vibrations. Used for focus and concentration spells and for success rituals.

- **Practical Magic**—the herb can be grown easily in pots and is a must-have addition to any witch's kitchen. It's an all-round additive for pick-me-up drinks and meals. When eaten regularly, it can help relieve nausea and headaches. Wonderful on its own or as an addition to any hot or cold herbal tea.

Witch's Brew

You will need to gather:

- a slice of lemon
- 2 cups of hot water
- 1 teaspoon of chamomile tea
- 1 teaspoon of orange marmalade
- 1 teaspoon of fresh mint or mint tea

Place all the ingredients in a teapot and pour in the hot water. Allow the brew to sit for 5 minutes as you repeat this incantation:

'Earth, Fire, Air and Sea, Natural Magic come to me.'

NUTMEG

- **Esoteric Magic**—stimulating vibration. Used for casting money and success spells.

- **Practical Magic**—ancient medicinal qualities for poor circulation and exhaustion. Go easy on how much you sprinkle onto food, as too much can be slightly hallucinogenic—which is exactly why it was often used in 'flying' formulas.

To make your own mild flying formula to give you a kick start for a successful day ahead, sprinkle a small amount into a yogurt milkshake and drink it early in the day. Take some nutmeg with you to work and sprinkle a little pinch of it around you in the afternoon before a big meeting.

ONIONS

- **Esoteric Magic**—highly protective and purifying vibrations, used in banishing spells and looking into the past.

- **Practical Magic**—the use of this plant is so ancient that it is said Hippocrates, the father of medicine, recommended onion juice as a curative for just about everything. Don't go so far as drinking the juice, but definitely try to use onion in lots of your cooking because it is a great blood cleanser, helps relieve water retention and aids the lymphatic system.

ORANGES

- **Esoteric Magic**—uplifting vibrations. Ruled by the power of the Sun, used in love, healing and pregnancy spells.

- **Practical Magic**—strengthens the heart and another great source of vitamin C.

Squeeze fresh orange juice at least once or twice a week for you and your family for a powerful dose of Sun power. To help stimulate fertile power, roll an orange softly over your tummy.

PARSLEY

- **Esoteric Magic**—stimulating and healing vibrations. Used for protection and family spells.

- **Practical Magic**—high in vitamins A and C, it has been used for centuries in the treatment of kidney and bladder problems as well as sciatica. It is said that parsley also helps to relieve labor pains, and it can be chewed after meals to freshen the breath.

PEPPER (BLACK AND WHITE)

- **Esoteric Magic**—banishing and cleansing vibrations. Used for both hexing and healing spells.

- **Practical Magic**—used for over 3,000 years in India and China as a food and in medicine as a treatment for heartburn, stiff muscles and colic.

Sprinkle it over food to stimulate appetite and to add zest and power to any savory dish.

ROSEHIPS

- **Esoteric Magic**—arousing and healing vibrations. Used in love potions and also wonderful for Fairy spells and rituals.

162

- ⊚ **Practical Magic**—the oil helps to heal scars and is a wonderful addition to skin cream. It can be purchased as a herbal tea and is a lovely healing drink for monthly cramps.

Fairy Basket

Place baskets of rosehips and geranium and lavender potpourri around your home to attract Fairy Magic and to have insightful dreams.

ROSEMARY

- ⊚ **Esoteric Magic**—probably one of the most important witchy plants (most old folk charmers would have a rosemary bush growing outside to protect the home). With high Magic and protective resonance, and good for just about every kind of spell, it adds power to most rituals.

- ⊚ **Practical Magic**—rosemary is an aid to digestion, clears the blood and liver and is a wonderful addition to hair and skin tonics. Always have a bunch hanging somewhere in the magical kitchen for both good luck and good health.

ROSES

- **Esoteric Magic**—arousing and passionate vibrations. Also has a sacred 'goddess' resonance. It was once the custom to suspend a rose over a conference or dinner table to bring truth and sacred energy to the conversation (hence the still-used 'ceiling rose'); also great for love and sexuality spells.

- **Practical Magic**—a blood cleanser and natural antiseptic agent with a wonderfully pleasant flavor. Used for centuries in food and medicines.

Rose-Petal Butter

You will need to gather:

- *1 cup of fresh red rose petals from roses that have been grown without pesticides*
- *a glass jar with a lid*
- *4 1/2 ounces (125 grams) of butter wrapped in waxed paper*
- *a few slices of white bread*

Sprinkle a layer of rose petals into the bottom of the jar, then put in the butter wrapped in waxed paper. Cover again with another layer of rose petals. Twist the lid of the jar on firmly and leave in the refrigerator or a cool room overnight. The stronger the scent of the roses, the better the flavor of the butter will be.

The next day, cut up some fresh white bread into finger-sized pieces or triangles, and spread generously with the scented butter as well as sprinkling more fresh petals between the slices and over the dish.

SALT

- ✺ **Esoteric Magic**—the use of salt in Magic goes way back to antiquity. Cleansing, protective and with high Magic resonance, it is used for clearing and banishing spells and to prepare altars and areas for all kinds of sorcery. A must-have in any witchy kitchen.

- ✺ **Practical Magic**—used in the olden days as a cleanser and antibiotic agent, still great in warm water as a gargle for sore throats and toothache. Adds taste to foods, but go easy as it does help to retain water.

Bless This House

Mix a pinch of rosemary and salt together in a bowl. Stand in the Magical hearth (the kitchen) of your home and walk in a widdershins (counterclockwise) direction just once around the room, sprinkling the mixture as you go.

Next, stand in the kitchen and relax your body and mind. Visualize the circle of salt mixture now expanding and growing outward so that your whole house or apartment is now encircled with cleansing energy.

After a moment or two, get your broom (preferably straw, of course!) and sweep up the mixture into a dustpan.

The very moment you awaken your search for Magical knowledge is the moment you consciously become a magician.

Prosperity Potions

GOOD LUCK AND MONEY OIL

Money and lottery spells will work best if you have lots of fun casting them, and then relax and let the universe take its course.

You will need to gather:

- $10 bill
- a clear quartz crystal
- lemongrass essential oil
- an eyedropper
- peppermint essential oil
- 1 small bottle of almond oil

On a Wednesday or the night of a New Moon, place the ten-dollar bill on a clean table and then place the clear quartz crystal on top. Put the rest of your spell items nearby on the table and then, with an eye dropper, put three drops each of the peppermint and lemongrass essential oils into the bottle of almond oil. Firmly screw the lid back onto the almond oil and start shaking the bottle quite vigorously as you say:

> 'Shake up, shake up spirits of money and wealth,
> take out, take out bad luck and now bring me success instead.'

Next, put the bottle back on the table, unscrew the lid and wipe a drop of the Magic oil onto the ten-dollar bill as well as a drop or two over the quartz crystal. Leave them overnight to be charged by the power of the Moon.

In the morning, put the ten-dollar bill back into your wallet and keep the money oil in a cool place to be used whenever you need to attract good fortune.

PROBLEM SOLVER

To make the correct decision concerning a problem, burn a mixture of sandalwood and frankincense essential oils in an oil burner and meditate until the right way forward is revealed to you.

SMELL THE ROSES

Sprinkle your clothing with rose water for a good day and good feelings.

Lottery Luck

Use this spell to bring prosperity and good fortune in the lottery. But keep in mind my Good Witch's rule for money Magic: 'Only gamble with money you can afford to lose.' In other words, lucky charms can only work if you just spend spare change and never dip into your savings.

You will need to gather:

- *a green cloth*
- *a green candle*
- *3 almonds*
- *a sheet of clean white paper*
- *a pyrite stone (available at crystal shops)*
- *a white candle holder*
- *a small bowl*

On a Monday evening, create a lucky altar in your living room by laying the cloth on a side table and then placing on top the pyrite stone the candle in the candle holder and the almonds in the bowl.

Write your chosen lottery numbers on the paper and place it into the bowl and then light the candle. For 10 minutes concentrate on seeing yourself with the winning ticket.

Breathe calmly and evenly and hold the pyrite in your hand as you say:

'Mother Earth, Father Fire, bring me what I desire. So Mote It Be.'

After you blow out the candle, leave the altar in place for at least a month or so and repeat the spell every Monday.

Winning Numbers

Invoke the power of lucky Jupiter to help you pick some winning numbers.

You will need to gather:

- ◎ peppermint incense
- ◎ a small piece of putty or Blu-Tac
- ◎ 1 ft (30 cm) of red cord
- ◎ 1 teaspoon of sage
- ◎ a sheet of white paper
- ◎ green paint or a green marking pen
- ◎ two small pebbles
- ◎ a sheet of red paper

One week before you buy your lottery ticket, light the incense and place the piece of white paper on a table along with the Blu-Tac and green paint or marker and the cord and sit comfortably nearby. Pick up the putty or Blu-Tac and roll it into a ball with your hands. Then press it with your left thumb and put a dab of green paint or pen on the thumbprint. Wrap up the ball with the red cord and, while you hold it carefully, repeat these words:

> 'With the Seal of Jupiter, by the power of Mercury,
> give me numbers on a count of three.'

Put down the ball and clap your hands three times and then write down the first numbers that come into your mind. Repeat the chant until you have as many numbers as you need, and leave the Magic ball near your money documents.

After you have purchased your lottery ticket, place it between the two pebbles. Then stand about 3 feet away with the sage in your right hand. Look toward the pebbles and sprinkle the sage in a clockwise direction around you as you repeat this incantation:

'Aradia, Fortuna, carry your winning way
toward me from this day.'

Finish the spell by wrapping up your lottery ticket in the red paper and saying:

'It Will Be So.'

This spell takes some time and patience but works like a charm to help you pick your Magic numbers.

The Luck of the Irish

An enchanting tradition for attracting luck with money is to make a cup of chamomile tea, allow it to cool completely and then place it in the refrigerator for an hour.

Wash your hands in the cold chamomile tea and wipe your hands with a clean towel as you say:

'With the luck of the Shamrock,
from times of old,
allow my path
to be paved with gold.'

For Good Fortune Fairies

Attract the Fairies of luck into your house by wiping down your front and back door with a white cloth that has been soaked in a mixture of 2 cups of spring water and 3 drops of tea-tree oil.

Wonderstones

The ancient Druids wore enchanted Adder Stones on their fingers or as a pendant to bring good luck and health. Adder Stones are made from a ring-shaped crystal or a stone with a natural hole in the middle.

For a powerful protection charm, find a piece of amber that contains some fossilized insects and keep it near your front door.

If you don't want to go to the expense of purchasing a special stone, keep your eye out for any oddly shaped or appealing pebbles on the ground, and keep the stone you choose in a drawstring bag as your own mystical 'Wonderstone'. (To ensure its lasting power, don't let anyone else touch it.)

Attracting Abundance

Have you ever heard of the affirmation, 'Money will come when I'm ready to receive it'? This spell will get you into a winning state of mind.

You will need to gather:

- a silver candle
- a few cloves
- some nutmeg
- a small bowl

On the night of a New or Growing Moon, light the candle and mix the nutmeg and cloves in the bowl.

As you feel yourself surrounded by positive thoughts and energy, repeat these Magic words:

'Artemis, Darius, call abundance to my vicinity.
Summon the call of prosperity,
as is my right, O Blessed Be.'

Blow out the candle after 20 minutes and bury the nutmeg and cloves near your front door.

New Year Magic

Instead of making the same old New Year resolutions, why not cast a lucky New Year spell instead.

As well as for the New Year, you can cast this spell on the ninth of any month at nine o'clock in the morning or night.

Light a gold candle and sit comfortably nearby while you relax your mind and body for a few moments. On a piece of purple paper, write down your wishes for the New Year nine times, then repeat these words:

> 'Copper, gold, silver, tin,
> as the year proceeds, my luck is in.'

Keep your wish list in a special place and make sure you read it regularly.

The Good Oil

To rid yourself of negative energy and bad luck, take a framed photo of yourself, place it face upward, and rub coconut oil over it.

The study of Magic
will allow you to open up
all the possibilities of the universe,
and encourage your own
human and spiritual development.

Beauty and Body Charms

Society puts a lot of emphasis on health and looks nowadays, and even though men and women come in a wonderful variety of beautifully natural shapes and sizes which are perfectly normal and healthy for them, many people feel stressed and pressured about their body image, or feel as if they need to lose weight really fast.

Of course, there is no Magic spell that is going to make you lose weight overnight so that, ZAP! you are suddenly a famous supermodel. But I do believe that true beauty and a good self-image do come from within and Magic can help with rituals to relax you and help you to learn to love yourself. Be proud and happy with whatever body the wonderful universe is lending you while you are here in this dimension, and enjoy this wonderful planet we call Mother Earth.

The following are a few self-esteem and healthy body spells to have fun with and to help to de-stress and maintain the greatest magical temple of all—your own god/dess-given body!

DEAR DIARY

Start up an enchanted diary by finding a new notebook and writing on the cover, 'My Wonderful Life'. Each day, write down at least one positive thing that happened to you during the day. It can be anything that makes you feel good, such as 'I saw a gorgeous sunset' or 'I had a productive day at work' or 'A young child smiled at me.' Read through the pages each week to keep yourself inspired and motivated.

Mirror Mirror

True beauty starts from within and radiates outwards to give you charisma and confidence.

Find some time for yourself when you can be alone for a while and take a relaxing warm shower or bath. After you have patted yourself dry, remain skyclad (the magical term for being naked) and stand in front of your bathroom mirror. Place a lightly scented body lotion nearby and start looking at your own reflection in the mirror, starting with your face, concentrating especially on your eyes. As you look into your eyes, repeat this incantation:

> 'Inside me beautiful Magic lives,
> my eyes are windows to an enchanted place.'

Next, smile a big smile and let yourself have a giggle or a laugh if you feel like it. Then put your hands softly up to touch your face and repeat this incantation:

> 'Inside me wonderful Magic lives,
> I can feel its glow when I touch my face.'

Then, squeeze some of the lotion onto your palms and rub it gently over your entire body, feeling yourself being filled with positive energy and power. When you are ready to get dressed, seal the spell's Magic with these words:

> 'I will honor myself and my glorious mind, spirit and body.'

Superbody

Cook up this enchanted brew to help you curb your appetite for junk food.

You will need to gather:

- 2 carrots
- a small bunch of celery
- 3 cups of spring water
- 3 tomatoes
- 1 sprig of parsley
- 1 sprig each of thyme and marjoram

Wash the vegetables and parsley well, then chop them up and place them in a saucepan with the spring water. Simmer for 10 minutes or until soft. Stir with a wooden spoon and sprinkle in the thyme and marjoram as you repeat this incantation:

> 'Here is energy and joy anew.
> Inspiring forces are in this brew.'

Allow the soup to cool, then strain the liquid into a bowl. As you throw the cooked vegetables into the garbage bin, say:

'There go my old worries and woe.'

Drink a cup of the Magic liquid before lunch or dinner. It can be stored in the refrigerator for just a day or two, then discard and make a fresh batch.

Good Habits

This spell works like a charm to get rid of any habits like smoking or niggling worries.

You will need to gather:

- ⊚ a cup
- ⊚ a white candle
- ⊚ sandalwood incense

Set the empty cup on a table in front of the candle. Light the incense and the candle and stand near the table as you pick up the cup in both hands and hold it high over the candle and incense.

Breathe slowly and evenly for a moment until you are calm and centered.

Then, hold the cup near your chest and slowly blow air into it, silently naming each bad habit and negative energy you wish removed from your life. When finished, turn the cup upside down onto the table, saying firmly:

> 'The contents of this vessel, I give up to thee,
> Lords of Light,
> exchange these bad habits for positive actions.'

Finish by blowing out the candle and incense and saying:

> 'It shall be done, O Blessed Be.'

THE TIME IS RIGHT

One of the most magical times to begin a new health regime is at the beginning of a Waning or Diminishing Moon (when the Moon is moving from full back to new). This will give a special boost to your bid for a fitter and healthier body.

LUNAR LOCKS

To help your hair grow long and lustrous, only trim it on a day or evening of a Full Moon.

Shiny Hair Hex

This is an old Hungarian beauty spell for gleaming hair and youthful energy.

You will need to gather:

- *rosemary essential oil*
- *a sheet of paper*
- *a sprig of rosemary*
- *olive oil*
- *a red pen*
- *a couple of glasses of spring or mineral water*

Blend 6 drops of rosemary essence in an ounce (25 ml) of olive oil. Massage the mixture into your hair, right down to the ends, while you close your eyes and inhale the scent. Write your name on the paper with the red pen and then dip the sprig of rosemary into a glass of spring water and chant:

> 'Flowery dew and mystic grove,
> bring health and beauty from above.'

Soak the paper in the spring water, removing it when the ink has faded. Wash the oil out of your hair with a natural shampoo and use a fresh glass of spring or mineral water as the final rinse. Bury the paper near a tree to enhance hair growth.

Good Vibrations

Some essences can be mixed with oils and worn on your body and clothes to attract good fortune and love. One of my favorite oils for mixing is almond, as it also possesses its own enchanted vibration and will help strengthen the energy of your chosen essence. The best time to mix up a magical body oil is on Monday, the day of the Moon, at 7 pm.

Whatever path of the Craft you choose to follow is correct for you because at its highest level, the Craft should always be a path of self-acceptance and freedom of spirit

Love and Sex Charms

Flower Power

This is a powerful charm to attract a lover toward you.

You will need to gather:

- ☺ hibiscuses (pick 3 mature flowers and 3 unopened buds)
- ☺ a white cloth
- ☺ a cup of red wine
- ☺ a pinch of thyme and a pinch of sage
- ☺ around 8 inches (20 cm) of copper wire.

Mix a pinch each of thyme and sage in a cup of red wine. Leave the mixture in the Sun for one day. When the Sun goes down, dip your finger into the mixture and use it to paint a stick figure onto the white cloth while you think about your intended lover. Then place all the hibiscus flowers on top of the cloth, roll it up and then tie the bundle up with the piece of copper wire. Next put it outside or near an open window and leave it to be charged by the light of the Moon overnight.

The next day unwrap the bundle, throw away the cloth and wire and bury the flowers near your front door.

Living Goddess

Enliven your bedroom with a 'living' figurehead for love and sexual energy.

You will need to gather:

- any sized statue (a small one is fine) of your favorite love god or goddess (e.g., Aphrodite, Venus, Pan, Hermes)
- a cup of almond, olive or jojoba oil
- a shot of vodka
- 1 each teaspoon of mugwort, geranium leaves, comfrey leaves or tea
- a teaspoon of ground coriander or finely chopped cilantro
- a sprinkle of salt

Grind or chop up your herbs and sprinkle them into a bowl along with a shot of vodka and leave them to sit for a few hours. Then pour a cup of almond, olive or jojoba oil on top. With a silver or wooden spoon scoop up three teaspoons of the oil and pour over the god or goddess as you say:

'Welcome to my temple, may you be always in comfort and peace within my home. With the blessing of Holda be now charged with the power of love.'

Then, sprinkle salt around the statue in a clockwise circle and say:

'With this earth you have physical form.'

Next blow breath onto the statue and say:

'With my breath, you shall breathe as I breathe.'

Light a candle and hold it near the statue and say:

'By this sacred fire you are enriched with the spark of life.'

Finally, wash the statue with water and say:

'By the great waters you come to us from across the sea of destiny.'

Finish by wiping the statue dry and sprinkling a few rose or gardenia petals on top and around it. Keep the statue on your altar or in a special area of your bedroom.

The Soulmate Special

To help bring your soulmate into your life.

You will need to gather:

- ◎ *a rose quartz crystal*
- ◎ *floral perfume*
- ◎ *a piece of red cloth*

Take the crystal and hold it close to your chest while you concentrate your thoughts on love and happiness. Feel your heart filling up with emotion as you say:

> 'With crystal clear spirit, through all eternity,
> I open my mind and heart to receive true love.
> So Shall It Be.'

Then spray the crystal with the perfume, wrap it in the cloth and keep it near your bed for one to three months.

Pleased To Meet Me

This is a perfect spell to cast if you wish to spark up a romance with either an old acquaintance or a new friend. You will need to first invite your intended lover over to your place and an hour or so before they arrive get dressed in something that contains the color blue.

You will need to gather:

- ◎ an oil burner (the kind that allows you to drop the oils into a water solution and then heat with a candle)
- ◎ 3 drops of sandalwood oil
- ◎ 3 drops of rose oil (you may substitute rose geranium if you wish)
- ◎ 3 drops of orange oil
- ◎ 3 drops of jasmine oil

Think about where you would like to entertain your guest and then take the ingredients and oil burner into the chosen room. Next, pour a little water into the oil burner and then, one by one, pour in the drops of the different oils. Light the oil burner candle and then say:

'I welcome the warm spirits of my home, and may we be surrounded by feelings of romantic love, may his (her) heart be opened and inspired, O Blessed Be.'

Then go and get ready. Allow the aroma to permeate the room for at least an hour before he or she arrives. (You can also leave the mixture on while they are visiting you, but make sure you turn off the oil burner if you leave the house.)

Circles of Love

To encircle you in waves of love and to attract your chosen one toward you, cast this powerful spell either on a Friday or on the night of a Full Moon.

You will need to gather:

- ◎ *a white plate*
- ◎ *a bottle of basil essential oil*
- ◎ *a bottle of lemon essential oil*
- ◎ *a bottle of musk essential oil*
- ◎ *a white candle and a red candle*

Find a table or a flat surface to lay all your ingredients on. Put the two candles in holders on either side of the white plate (the white candle on the left and the red on the right) and light both candles.

Think about the person you want to attract toward you and in your mind's eye imagine you see their reflection inside the plate. Next, with the first bottle of essential oil (basil), dab a little bit on your forefinger and wipe a clockwise circle of oil around the entire edge of the plate while you say:

> 'With the power of one, I cast this circle of love.'

Then do the same thing with the second bottle of oil (lemon), and while wiping a clockwise circle around the plate say:

> 'With the power of two, I cast this circle of love.'

And finally pick up the last bottle of essential oil (the musk) and wipe a third circle around the plate, while you say:

> 'With the power of three, the circles are cast, the love will last. So Shall It Be.'

Blow or snuff out the candles and leave the plate in a safe place for seven days. (Straight after the ceremony throw away the cotton bud and make sure you wash your hands well to remove all residues of the essential oils, and don't put the oils anywhere near your eyes, as they are very potent.) After seven days, the spell's power will have been sent out into the universe to do its work, so you can then wash the plate in soap and water and use it as normal.

Sexagram

Witchcraft is one of the few spiritual paths that does not separate spirituality from sexuality. In fact, many traditions of the Craft celebrate the merging of the body, mind and spirit and the raising of magical power during the sacred act of sex.

The beautiful and powerful sex rite can be performed to enhance erotic passion between you and your partner, and as an added bonus, the sexual energy raised during lovemaking can be used to empower any type of spell.

You will need to gather:

- some pillows and cushions
- a handful of rose petals
- a few candles
- a double bed sheet
- musk incense
- massage oil of your choice (such as almond or jojoba)

Choose a private room where you can create a magical boudoir for the ritual. Clean an area of the floor and lay down a double bed sheet (it can be in any of your favorite colors). Then lay plenty of cushions and pillows on top and sprinkle a large circle of rose petals (or frangipanis) around everything in a clockwise direction. Dim the lights, put on some sexy background music if you like, and then light the musk incense.

Next, go and have a bath or shower together with your partner; take your time washing and languishing in the warm water, and when you are both fully relaxed and ready, pat each other dry and, remaining skyclad, walk back hand in hand into your magical boudoir. If you like, you can light a few candles in the room for extra atmosphere. Whenever you are ready, go and stand on either side of the circle of pillows so you are facing each other with your arms and legs apart. Looking directly into each other's eyes, begin reciting these incantations.

The woman's first words are:

'Arise O Herne, Hu Gadern.'

The man then answers:

'I am Herne, your horned god, your stag has risen
from the sacred woodlands.'

The woman answers:

'Herne, you are my stag, you are my ram, my sacred temple
is moist and open, come and let's ignite the astral flame.'

Then both come into the circle and get comfortable on the pillows and start kissing and caressing and anointing each other's bodies with the massage oil (almond or jojoba or one of your own choosing).

The rest of this powerfully potent ritual is up to your own sexy imagination, but if you do want to use the raised energy for magic during your lovemaking, then when either or both of you are at the point of orgasm, focus your mind on the purpose of your spell to help send it zooming off into the Universe.

FERTILITY MAGIC

Since time began, women have been making lucky charms and casting fertility spells to help them conceive their dream baby.

Many of these old traditions follow the cycles of the Sun and the Moon, as well as the connection between Mother Nature and Goddess Magic. The ancient spellcasters observed that the Moon has a definite link to female fertility and created many charms that could harness the power of the goddess Luna.

Remember that the female cycle usually follows the 13 lunar months. Find out when your monthly ovulation time is and perform this spell then.

You will need to gather:

- ꧁ *apple-scented body cream*
- ꧁ *a silver necklace*

Take a relaxing shower (ideally a romantic one with your partner) and then, with your partner, gently massage the apple-scented body cream into your skin, paying extra attention to your tummy area. Imagine as you rub in the cream that your and your partner's hands are glowing with a mystic silver light that is filling this area with life and power. Actually visualize yourself pregnant as your partner gently places the necklace around your neck and you repeat these Magic words together:

'Silvery goddess, o shining Luna,
I wear your precious light.
Let fertile power glow through me.
O Blessed Be This Night.'

FERTILE PHASES

Many Celtic magicians believe that a woman is most fertile for the three days around the same phase of the Moon as she was born under. In other words, if you were born during a New Moon, then you should be most fertile during a New Moon; if you were born during a Full Moon, you are most fertile during that time.

Love Potion

Excellent for spells of romance and fertility.

You will need to gather:

- romantic music
- red wine or fruit drink
- geranium essential oil
- 2 gold-colored goblets
- gardenia and rose petals
- an oil burner

Have some sexy fun by casting this spell with your partner. At midnight on a Friday, take a shower together and both dress in light clothing. Play some romantic music and fill the goblets with the wine or fruit drink. Prepare the bedroom beforehand by scattering the flower petals over the freshly made bed. Burn the geranium essence and, after you each take a sip from the goblets, repeat this incantation:

> 'Bacchus, god of wine and fun, Make our wishes come true
> And fill our days with wonder.'

If you wish to conceive a child, an ancient Sun ritual for babymaking is to place some yellow feathers and an orange scarf under the bed before you make love.

A BOY OR A GIRL?

For centuries it has been recognized that astrological signs tend to have either a masculine or feminine nature. To help you choose the sex of your baby, buy a calendar that shows the 12 astrological phases and cast your fertility spell during the best star time to conceive either a boy or a girl.

For a boy, choose Masculine Signs

Aries
Gemini
Leo
Libra
Sagittarius
Aquarius

For a girl, choose Feminine Signs

Taurus
Cancer
Virgo
Scorpio
Capricorn
Pisces

A Little Ray of Sunshine

In all cultures, the Sun has been revered and honored as the bringer of life and fertile energy. Connect with the eternal power of Apollo, the Sun god, by casting this spell at noon at the beginning of the most fertile time of the month for you.

You will need to gather:

- a white tablecloth
- a few seashells
- a vase of yellow rosebuds
- c bay leaf

Prepare a love altar in your bedroom by placing the tablecloth and rosebuds on a table or your dresser along with the seashells.

Hold the bay leaf—which is also ruled by the Sun—in your hand for a few moments while you sit calmly near your altar. Gaze at the rosebuds and visualize them starting to open and bloom. As you do this, imagine that your whole body is blooming and opening up like a beautiful flower, and repeat this incantation:

> 'Golden Apollo, from this enchanted hour,
> let me open to fertile seed,
> help me receive love's Magic power.'

To seal the spell's power, place the bay leaf under your pillow before you make love with your partner.

Enchanted Sun Kisses

Each week on the day of the Sun (Sunday), sit outside in the light or near an open window and roll an orange around your tummy as you say:

'Sun kissed with Nature's bliss
help me to conceive.'

Then kiss the orange three times, cut it into quarters and eat it with breakfast or lunch.

Special Seeds

Another old Magic charm is for couples to sprinkle uncooked rice or sunflower seeds under the marital bed to aid fertility.

Basil For Babies

Add a Magic dash of basil to your dinner to spice up your chances of conception.

Once you learn to

tap into your

inner power,

it can really

change your life.

Dream Weaver

The ancient alchemists understood that 'when the body sleeps the soul awakens' and that our dreams are a magical source of inspiration, guidance and prophecy. Dreams are just like secret messages from our spiritual self. They give us information on what is really happening deep in our subconscious mind and the universe around us. With these dream spells and enchanted rituals you can also learn to tap into the power of your dreams—to show you how to best deal with everyday problems and to give you important insights into the past and the future.

Remembering Your Dreams

We can all learn how to remember our dreams more clearly by following these mind-power and focusing techniques.

200

First, make sure that you go to sleep in a quiet environment, without the interference or distraction of outside noises. If you do fall asleep while watching TV or listening to the radio, your dreaming pattern will take on some of what you have seen and heard, and will not be a real insight into your subconscious.

Start a Dream Workbook. Put a new diary and pen near your bed and as soon as you wake up in the morning write down immediately any images or emotions you had while you slept.

Before you go to sleep, sit on your bed and breathe calmly and deeply for a moment or two to relax and then repeat this incantation:

> 'Peace and understanding flow this night,
> O Universe, let me remember my dreams
> and clear my second sight.'

Dream Numbers

Half an hour or so before you go to bed, sit on a chair in front of a mirror and look at your own reflection as you repeat this incantation:

> 'I am grateful for life,
> and I know that wealth and prosperity
> are within me.'

Then, on a notepad, write down all of the numbers from one to 100 as you breathe calmly and let go of worries and stress. Turn over the page so you have a clean, new piece of paper and, as you get into bed, place the notebook and a pen nearby so you can easily write down any numbers that come to you in your dreams.

Sleepy Solutions

You know that old saying 'Go and sleep on it'? Well, it is true that while we sleep we can call on our higher wisdom to help make big decisions and solve all sorts of problems.

To do this, before you go to bed write your problem or question on a red piece of paper. Sit in a quiet place, hold the paper in front of you, and gaze at the color of the paper and the words you have written.

Don't think about your problem or anything else; relax your mind and let yourself absorb the warmth and vibrancy of the color.

Then, just before you lie down, tear the paper into pieces and sprinkle them and some chamomile tea leaves under your bed. In the morning you will start to feel an answer to your important question forming.

An old Celtic charm for insightful dreams is to sprinkle salt under the four corners of the bed and walk clockwise around your bedroom three times with your question in mind.

Wealthy Dreaming

To bring forth dreams of wealth and insights into career direction, cast this spell on the night of a New or Full Moon.

Place some white carnation petals and geranium leaves under your pillow and say:

> 'Shasheeta, goddess of the mystic light,
> lead me to my rightful path.
> Show me the way
> to my rightful abundance and prosperity.'

Repeat this spell once a week for the next month.

Enchanted Dream Herbs

There are a few wonderful old herbs that can help you achieve many things while dreaming—like flying, astral traveling and visualizing your soulmate.

Before you go to bed, put a teaspoon or a teabag of the chosen herb into a cup of hot water and let it steep for 5 minutes. As you sip your tea, imagine that your body is feeling lighter and more tranquil.

- *Rosehip: superb for love and soulmate dreaming*
- *Valerian: wonderful for deep, healing dreams*
- *Mulberry: for dreams of flying and astral travel*

No Nightmares Elixir

A Magic potion to guard against nightmares can be made by mixing a teaspoon of apple-cider vinegar and a teaspoon of honey into a small cup of warm water and sipping this elixir slowly before bedtime.

Facing Your Demons

Whenever you have dreams about being chased, try to find the courage to stop running, and turn to face your pursuer. You will find that it's actually yourself and your inner fears trying to be understood and resolved.

Viewing The Future

To evoke dreams of future gazing and prediction, wear an amethyst crystal or moonstone on a chain or leather strap around your neck at night.

Dream Symbols

The memorable images and pictures in your dreams often hold hidden meaning and cosmic messages.

You will often have one main teaching dream each night, and these are a few of the symbols that may appear:

MALE AND FEMALE FIGURES:
represent your masculine and feminine sides

ROOMS IN A HOUSE OR APARTMENT:
represent the different chambers of your subconscious and memories

CHILDREN AND BABIES:
represent your inner child needing to be listened to

ANIMALS:
represent the different feelings you have about a situation (for instance, a wolf or shark would represent danger, a snake or horse usually suggests passion and sexuality)

A PET OR A RELATIVE WHO HAS PASSED AWAY:
you are about to receive important news

In Magic nothing is impossible!

It is really just a matter of spending time

learning and applying the natural laws of the universe on a daily basis.

Wikid Ways

There is nothing like a cup of brew, a hex and a well deserved rest. I'd recommend it to anyone who's had a hard day at the office, or has been stuck in bumper-to-bumper traffic.

HIGH-HEELED HEXER

There are times when you may experience some unwanted 'shadow passing', which is when other people either consciously or unconsciously pass their own dark shadows and fears over to us. You may be especially vulnerable to this during or after a relationship breakup. Cast this spell if you feel as if an ex-friend or lover has been sending you their dark shadows or especially when you have been left emotionally bruised and traumatized by a messy breakup.

You will need to gather:

- ⊚ for women: you will need a pair of red or black high-heeled shoes (stilettos are perfect)
- ⊚ for men: you can wear a pair of boots (cuban heel or cowboy boots are great, but any boots will do)
- ⊚ a photograph of the 'shadow passer' or a piece of paper and a pen.

At the stroke of midnight during a Waning Moon or Diminishing Moon, take the photograph or write the name of the shadow passer on the piece of paper three times and go to a private place where you will be undisturbed. Get completely undressed. Remain skyclad and put on your high-heeled shoes or boots. Keep the lights on and go and stand in front of a mirror. Look at your reflection in the mirror and breathe very calmly and deeply, concentrating only on positive and uplifting thoughts.

Next, take the photograph or the piece of paper, and put it down on the floor. Stand over it with your legs apart so you are directly over the picture and looking down at it, and then say these words with conviction:

'A woman (man) scorned is a sight to behold,
A woman's (man's) fury can turn fire cold,
When I gave you my sweet love
you gave me your deepest shadow,

208

But now at my feet your shadow I see
And I name and return it straight back
from whence it came.'

Then stamp on the photo or paper three times with your left heel and then three times with your right heel. When you've done that, stand with your arms raised and, looking to the heavens, say:

'Your shadow is finally released from me
and may it now return and serve you
in the name of love and good will,
O Blessed Be.'

To finish, throw the photo or paper into the garbage bin, and then go and either soak in a warm bath or have a refreshing shower to cleanse any leftover tensions and negative energy. Then go to bed for a well-deserved and restful night's sleep.

Home Protection

You will need to gather:

- 🌀 a mirror
- 🌀 fresh white sheets and coverlet
- 🌀 a handful of sage
- 🌀 some white flowers (such as daisies or gardenias) in two vases

To help the energy of your home flow properly, place the mirror on the back inside wall of your living room and, while holding the sage in your hand, walk clockwise around the main rooms of the house three times with your mind focused on positive thoughts as you repeat this incantation:

> 'Love before me, love beside me, love behind me,
> bring peace, harmony and truth.'

Make your bed with the fresh sheets and coverlet and place the flowers in your living room and bedroom.

It is also helpful to paint the front doors or windowsills light blue and to place some red carnations in a flower pot near the front entrance.

Give Up the Ghost

If you think there may be some strange energies in your home or you feel there may even be a leftover spirit or ghost, cast this 'happy ghost' spell.

On the stroke of midnight, light a white candle, hold a cup of spring water and sit in front of a mirror as you gaze in silence into the reflected light. Breathe in deeply a few times and then call the Angel of the Air, Earth, Water and Fire by sprinkling a few drops of the water around you and repeating this incantation:

> 'Heavenly angels hear my request,
> release those spirits from their earthly bounds.'

Concentrate on happy thoughts and, as you blow out the candle, say:

'And now you are at rest, it will be so, O Blessed Be.'

Happy Halloween

Halloween, or Allhallows Eve, was one of the most important festivals in old Europe for magicians and spellcasters because midnight on October 31 was traditionally when everyone counted their blessings for the year and the spirit world and the 'real' world got together for a big party. In ancient Europe it was called Samhain, and marked the end of one Druid year and the beginning of the next. Nowadays, Halloween is celebrated everywhere, and many children and adults have lots of fun dressing up as witches and goblins or their favorite characters from Hollywood movies. In Australia and elsewhere in the Southern Hemisphere many witches celebrate Halloween and Samhain on April 30. Whatever day you choose to follow to help you get into the celebratory spirit of Halloween, here are some spells and Magic tips to make your party memorable.

During the day of Halloween pick 13 leaves from a tree—one for each of the 13 Full Moons—and place them in a wooden or cardboard box as you recite this Halloween chant:

'O gracious goddess, I thank you for all your bounty,
as the wheel turns, walk with me from season to season
through night and day.'

Then place the box somewhere in your bedroom, maybe under your bed. This will ensure that you have lots of love and prosperity during the coming year.

In ancient times, Halloween was ruled by the goddess Pomona whose symbol is the fruit tree. To invoke the healing and loving energy of Pomona, cast this Magic apple spell at noon or midnight.

Cut up an apple into nine equal parts. Eat eight of the segments and then throw the ninth over your left shoulder as you say:

> 'Spirits and Magic fairies and elves,
> send good fortune to all our friends.'

If you're thinking of having a Halloween party, here are some tricks and treats for your guests to have fun with.

Keep the lights low and hang lots of party lanterns and fairy lights.

Set up a gypsy table in a corner of the room, complete with a crystal ball or a tarot card reader, and watch how many of your guests line up for a reading.

Many party shops sell spray-on fake cobwebs and plastic flying bats, both of which create a fabulous atmosphere in hallways. Hang some over the front door as well.

Bang tambourines and ring bells as a traditional way to celebrate Halloween. These instruments are often used by mediums to help bring friendly spirits into a room.

Make your own witch's broomstick by tying up one or more straw brooms with red, white and green ribbons. Then sweep your front doorstep with each of the brooms to help get rid of old problems and worries. Leave the brooms near the front and back doors during the party for good luck.

No Halloween party is complete without some Jack O'Lantern pumpkins placed in a window or lined up along the garden path. If you want to go all out, scoop out the inside of the pumpkin and carve in a smiling face. A much easier way is to paint a smiling face on the outside, then scoop out the middle. For extra effect you can burn a tealight candle inside while you recite:

> 'With this candle and by its light
> I welcome ye Spirits this Halloween night.'

To get you and your guests into a party mood, serve some homemade enchanted Halloween Lemon Wine.

Pour a bottle of white wine into a punch bowl. Add one large carton of lemonade and stir with a wooden spoon as you say:

> 'Bring joy and lightness on Allhallows Eve,
> begin the Magic on Halloween.'

Then slice up three or four lemons and add to the wine mixture along with a packet of maraschino cherries.
Serve chilled with ice in long glasses.

Broken Mirror

If you break a mirror, sprinkle salt and rosemary over the pieces, sweep them up carefully and throw them into the wastebasket. Then light a stick of sandalwood incense and walk counterclockwise around the wastebasket seven times as you say:

'One year gone of bad luck,
now two, three, four, five, six and seven.'

Then walk clockwise around the wastebasket as you say:

'Powers of the Universe, bring good fortune for one year, and
two, three, four, five, six and seven.
So Be It.'

Wands of Merlin

This fun party game uses 'wands' similar to divining sticks. The Wands of Merlin are made from small pieces of wood and are excellent tools for looking into the future and obtaining a quick yes or no answer to an important question.

Collect seven wooden sticks of exactly the same length (skewers or chopsticks will do fine).

Make a space on the floor of one of the party rooms for a large piece of white cardboard that has a straight line drawn straight across the middle. Stand at least 1 foot

(30 cm) away from the straight line and hold all of the sticks in your right hand. Close your eyes as you think about your important question. When you are ready, open your eyes and quickly throw the sticks toward the line drawn on the cardboard. Next, count how many sticks are above the line and how many are below. If there are more above the line, your answer is yes, if there are more below, your answer is no.

Soul Serenity

A magical time for rest and reflection, and for this self-esteem booster.

On the day of a Full or New Moon, revive your aura by dabbing on some orange essential oil in a little carrier oil and dressing in some mauve or purple clothing. Sit in front of an open window and breathe in and out deeply for a few moments to calm your body and mind. Rest your hands on your knees with your palms facing upward and repeat this incantation:

'Deep within me, my soul is my guide.
I shall put away my fears and know
that I deserve to fulfil my dreams
and follow my true purpose.
I open my mind and heart
in the flow of universal love.
O Blessed Be.'

Leave Me Be

Cast this spell to banish any negative energies or to protect you from bothersome people.

You will need to gather:

- 1 cup of white flour
- a piece of paper
- some old potato skins
- a garbage bag
- 1 cup of goat's milk or yogurt
- a pen
- a piece of fish

On the night of a Full or Diminishing Moon, make some dough using the flour and goat's milk or yogurt, kneading it until you have a firm mixture. Take the piece of paper and write the name of the bothersome person three times, then press it into the middle of the dough. Roll the dough into a ball and place it and the potato skins and a piece of fish inside a garbage bag as you say:

'The powers that be
send me a sacred spell,
to leave me alone will do you well'.

Throw the garbage bag into the garbage bin while you concentrate on letting go of negative thoughts and worries.

Kid Power

Children live in quite a different world from most adults. They absorb life like a sponge, their active minds still fresh and full of wonder at the universe around them. This is the time in their lives when they really should be encouraged to believe in their dreams and their own creative abilities. But nowadays, with the rise of technology, computer games and too much television, children can start to lose valuable play time in which to practice their natural fantasies and intuition. With these simple Magic rituals and games, you will not only bring out the imagination and self-expression of your child, but may also rediscover your own wonderful enchanted world.

Magical Beginnings

This is a beautiful way to bring Magic to a child's christening or baby-naming ceremony. You will use items that represent the four magical elements: Earth, Water, Fire and Air.

You will need to gather:

- a white candle
- a bowl of earth
- a bowl of spring water
- a white feather

Begin the ceremony by placing the four items on a table. Light the candle and hold the feather in your right hand as you look over toward the family gathering and say:

> 'Hail and welcome.
> We have come together to celebrate the naming of this precious
>   child.
> By Water and Earth you shall love the animals
>   and learn the wisdom of Nature.
> By Fire and Air, you will walk safely through all places.
> May the Universal Spirit, God and Goddess bless and protect you
>   as you grow in the light of love.'

Sweet Dreams

To help your child sleep peacefully and have pleasant dreams, create a tranquil and calming environment in her bedroom.

The windows should have light-colored, pastel-toned curtains and walls, and the headboard should be well away from the door. Cleanse the atmosphere by holding some vanilla incense and walking through the room with a peaceful mind and heart. At bedtime, turn off anything distracting or disturbing, such as the TV, loud music or radios. Put a lavender sachet under your child's pillow and, as you tuck her into bed, say:

> 'Feather light on starry night,
> cozy warm and tired,
> pleasant dreams and sweetest thoughts
> as little angels smile.'

Enchanted Birthday

Children's birthday parties are a perfect time for wishing spells and lucky charms. After all, we all still practice the ancient tradition of making a wish as we blow out our birthday candles.

To add a special touch of Magic to the celebration, fill the room with lots of balloons in your child's favorite color tied with green and white ribbons for luck. To help attract good fortune and fairy Magic, sprinkle glitter and rose petals or scented pot-pourri around the table.

Hang a mirror somewhere on the wall so the elves can see the food and drinks, and don't forget lots of cupcakes covered with sprinkles.

For extra enchantment, remember that pixies are supposed to be very fond of lemonade, strawberries and small bells.

You can also buy a Magic wishing book for your child and place it near the front door. Each of the party guests should sign their name in the book, near the words:

'As your birthday guest and friend so true,
I say your wishes will come true.'

Magic Wand

What could be more fabulous for a child than to have a Magic wand? Instead of buying one, help the child make his or her own special wand, which will be more effective.

Go outside together to a garden or park (preferably on a Sunday or on the morning of a Growing Moon) and search for a slim stick that appeals to your child. Hazel or hawthorn is the ancient traditional wood, but if you can't find these trees you can use the Druid's favorite, a twig from an oak tree. If you live in the Southern Hemisphere, you can use a stick from one of the native species for a highly effective Magic tool.

Take the stick home and let the child really use their imagination to decorate it with beads and feathers (or anything he or she wishes) tied on firmly with white, purple or gold string. You could also show the child how to glue on some stars and moons and lots of glitter. When finished, leave the wand near a window for one day and one night to absorb the light of the Sun and Moon. Then let the child charge it with his or her own personal Magic by holding it in the air and turning clockwise in a circle and saying:

*'I charge this wand for the good of all
in the name of love and Magic.'*

Tossing Cares Away

If your child is being bothered at school or is not getting along with some other kids, try this lovely charm.

Take some cotton balls, sprinkle them with a tiny dash of talcum powder, and have your child sit in a quiet, light-filled space while breathing calmly and letting her mind and body relax. Ask her to close her eyes and then put a few of the cotton balls in her hands and let her feel the softness of the fluffy cotton and gently breathe her cares away. Next, ask her to repeat after you these words:

'Softer, lighter, one, two, three,
problems float away from me.
I have friends who care about me
and I am as lucky as can be.'

Then, open a door or a window and help your child to throw the cotton balls outside, just as if she were throwing away all her worries and cares.

Self-esteem Builder

I receive many letters from parents and their children who are concerned about passing their school exams. This self-esteem charm will help release stress and give them the ability to focus on their studies.

You will need to gather:

- ⚬ *a mirror*
- ⚬ *a clear quartz crystal*
- ⚬ *a crayon or old lipstick*

On any morning or evening, have your child sit in front of a mirror so he can see his own reflection. Put the crystal on a table or flat surface nearby. Ask him to think about what he would like to achieve in the future or in his exams, and let him write that on the mirror surface. Next, ask him to concentrate on looking at himself in the mirror and let go of all worries so he feels calm and positive, and then repeat these words:

'I am unique and special,
I am loved by the Universe
and I have a clever mind.
When I believe in myself,
I can create wonderful things around me,
I can do anything and I believe in me.'

He can then keep the crystal in his room or school bag so he can repeat this spell whenever he feels like it.

The beauty of Magic is that you can weave your spells and charms wherever and whenever you want to.

Animal Magic

Most people adore their pets, especially their cats and dogs. And Nature lovers and Good Witches (including me) are no exception. As well as being great company, cats and dogs are quite psychic and can sense with uncanny accuracy when their owners need some extra love and affection. Without any prompting they will often know when family members are about to arrive home or need some extra protection. We consider our pets to be part of our family, so why not cast a few Magic spells to help keep them healthy and happy?

One of the most enchanted days of the week to cast pet spells is on Saturday, the day of Saturn, because it rules over Nature and its cycles. Another especially Magic time is when the moon is in the Earth signs of Capricorn, Virgo and Taurus.

Animal Protection

To keep good energy and healthy vibrations around your cat or dog, buy a cat's-eye crystal and a moonstone from a crystal shop and wash them in spring water on the day of a New, or Growing, Moon. Dry the stones thoroughly with a clean, white cloth. Hold the stones in your right hand and walk clockwise three times around your pet, softly repeating this incantation:

'Magico Mystico, bring forth your circle of power,
protect my beloved (say the name of your pet)
from this day on and every hour. O Blessed Be.'

Then keep the stones in a glass or earthenware jar near your front door.

Doggy Patrol

Is your pooch a wanderer? If so, you can draw in some protective energy by making a special charm for him to wear.

The color brown is good for animals, as it soothes their auras, so buy your dog a brown collar, preferably made of leather, and as you place it around his neck, say:

'San Francesco, protect this animal from harm.'

Then, before you attach his identification tag to the collar, hold the tag in your hand and focus your mind on seeing a warm, happy glow around him as you repeat this incantation:

*'While you wear this charm
may you never stray far from home.'*

Communicating With Your Cat

Cats have been known for centuries as psychic and mystical creatures, and your family kitty is no exception. If you'd like to know what your cat is thinking or to perhaps bring him or her into your Magic circle, try this spell at midnight on the night of a Full Moon.

You will need to gather:

- *a handful of aniseeds*
- *a mortar and pestle or a wooden bowl and spoon*
- *1 teaspoon of valerian tea leaves*
- *a small cotton or cheesecloth square*
- *some blue ribbon*

Place your spell items on a table, grind the aniseeds with the mortar and pestle or the bowl and spoon, and then mix in the valerian tea as you recite the words:

> 'By the eye of the cat,
> by the wing of the bat,
> be clean and clear.
> Bring the familiar spirit near.'

Finish your spell by pouring the mixture onto the cheesecloth and tying up the ends with the ribbon. Wear this bag in your pocket when you're playing with your cat or simply hang it near its bed.

Fly Away Fleas

An old charm to keep your dog or cat free from fleas is to pour two cups of mineral water into a bowl and mix in one drop each of sage, cedar and fennel essential oils. Stir the potion counterclockwise with a wooden spoon as you say these Magic words aloud:

> 'Fly away fleas, begone I say,
> don't come back another day!'

Then sprinkle some of the mixture directly over your pet's coat or onto a brush and comb carefully over its entire fur.

Healing Spell

When your trusted dog or cat has to visit the vet, you can cast this charm to help speed up the healing or to calm its nerves.

Light some sandalwood incense and a brown and green candle. Sit quietly nearby with your pet and speak quietly to it and gently stroke its fur for a few moments. As you do this, say the name of the animal goddess Bast (for a cat) or Brigit (if it's a dog) nine times, and then say:

> 'I call on the guardian Goddess
> to care and protect this animal.
> Bring health and comfort
> and allow them to be well in the eyes
> of Nature.'

Pet Charms

Catnip: helps create a bond between you and your cat; place it in a wooden box or in a drawstring pouch when you are playing together.

Vervain: scatter over your garden or footpath to quiet a barking dog.

Meditating Kitty

For a more spiritual and tranquil cat, sprinkle some catnip and oregano into a brown drawstring bag and make a smaller sachet for your cat. Wear yours for three days around your neck while you are meditating with your puddy for at least 15 minutes a day. You can either tie the pet's sachet to its collar while you meditate, or place it near the cat. After those three days, take all the herbs and throw them into the wind at midday or midnight.

If you wish to try this with your dog, use rosemary instead of catnip and add a dash of chamomile.

Power Paws

An old folk charm to help stop a straying pet is to rub a little pure butter onto its front paws once a month during a Full or New Moon.

If you are going on holiday and you have to leave your pet with friends or at a boarding kennel, be sure to pack a photo of you and your pet together, along with one or two of their hairs in a matchbox. This is said to stop them fretting for you too much.

The beauty of Magic is that you can weave your spells and charms wherever and whenever you want to.

Broomstick Travel

Are you just itching to get away on a romantic weekend for two? Or perhaps a trip on your own around the world is your idea of seventh heaven. Whether you dream of lazing on a tropical island or kicking up your heels in a big city, you can help make your dreams come true by weaving a little travel Magic.

Neptune's Wish

If your wish is to go on a fabulous holiday near the sea, cast this spell at mid-day on a Sunday.

Stand near a pond or a stretch of water, holding a ginger root and some seaweed in your hand. Try to focus your mind on where you would like to go and, as you gaze into the water, repeat this incantation:

'By the power of Neptune,
by the Gods of the sea.
Grant me a good journey
and so shall it be.'

Throw the ginger and the seaweed into the water; then close your eyes and imagine that you are already on your holiday by the sea, smelling the salty air, strolling along the beach and having a great time.

Bon Voyage Balm

To help make sure you are feeling healthy and fit for your holiday, perform this Magic ritual on either a day of a New Moon or a Sunday.

You will need to gather:

- 2 blue candles
- lavender essential oil
- bergamot essential oil (optional)
- a blue pen
- an oil burner
- rosemary essential oil
- a sheet of paper

Light the candles and oil burner, adding a few drops of the lavender and rosemary oils (and a few drops of bergamot to bring in more vibrations of healing). Stand to the right side of the room, raise your arms above your head and look up to the ceiling as you call in the positive energy forces by repeating this incantation:

'Great healing powers,
come directly to me,
fill me with strength and vigor.
In return I will send out
gratitude to the Universe.'

Next, take the piece of paper and use the blue pen to write down your travel destination and when you plan to go. Read this through a few times and then say with confidence:

'As I prepare for my trip
I will be well and fit.'

Leave the candles and oils burning for another minute or two, then as you blow them out, say:

'It Will Be So.'

Traveling Star

If you or a loved one is going away, cast this protection charm for a safe and happy journey.

Seven days before the trip, put seven hazelnuts into a green cloth and tie up the ends with a piece of string while you focus on positive and happy thoughts and repeat this incantation:

'One, my wish is for safe traveling,
two, my wish is for a comfortable ride,
three, my wish is for an interesting journey,
four, my wish is for good weather,
five, my wish is for happiness,
six, my wish is for wonderful memories,
and seven, Oh Traveling Star, guide us all safely home.'

Then place the pouch into one of the luggage bags and sprinkle a pinch of salt over all the rest of the luggage for luck.

Jetsetter

If you suffer from fear of flying, then take these charms with you on your flight. Hold on to them whenever you need some strength and tranquillity.

A week or so before you go on your trip, collect a piece of amber, a clear quartz, and a tiger's-eye or cat's-eye crystal (available at crystal shops) and leave them soaking in a glass of milk for one night.

In the morning, wash them with mineral water and, after drying them thoroughly, hold them in your hands and repeat this incantation:

> 'Hermes, Pegasus, Gods of Luck and Flight,
> protect me from this moment
> and guide the plane through darkness and light.'

Take the crystals with you in a blue pouch and you'll be up there with the rest of the jetsetters in no time.

Magic Planet

Confused about where you should go on your trip? Cast this spell at 10 am on any day.

Gather around you some magazine clippings and travel brochures of exotic and exciting locations from around the world. Then find a Y-shaped branch from a tree. After you have placed the pictures around you in a semicircle, grasp the short ends of the branch with your hands and allow the long end to tip downward near the brochures as you say:

> 'Apollo and Zeus guide me now
> as this branch shows me how,
> inspiration shall be here
> to adventure I will steer.'

Close your eyes for a moment and let the branch move from side to side. When you feel a strong pull in any direction, stop the branch there and open your eyes to see your travel destination revealed.

Magic Travel Tips

For some enchanting gift ideas for traveling friends, try to find copies of old maps of the world or an old-style compass. Velvet or cotton shoe bags in lucky colors such as green and blue also make magical presents.

To empower your gifts, buy them on Wednesday, the day of the God of journeys and communication, Mercury.

To help boost your own holiday finances, gather green clover on the night or day of a New Moon and sprinkle in a circle around your bank statements.

To attract money and savings, each day before your trip wrap a one-dollar coin in silver foil and put it inside an old money purse that has been dusted with a pinch of cinnamon.

Business Booster

Not all journeys are for holidays. If you're going on an important business trip, give yourself a bit of extra luck on the way.

Before you leave on your trip, bless your credit cards and business documents with this lucky spell.

Cast your Magic on a Sunday, preferably in the sunlight. The Sun encourages more 'gold' and can help attract success into your life. Gather together your documents and cards and wrap them in a bright yellow or gold-colored scarf. Place the bundle on a flat surface, light a stick of frankincense and wave it over the bundle as you visualize your future business meeting. Keep your thoughts positive and upbeat as you repeat this incantation:

'Solar Magic here begins,
from Apollo's chariot flies
success to win.'

Fly Away

There are some ancient recipes for 'flying ointment' that were used for broomsticks, but since we are modern Magic Spinners, we much prefer traveling by jet. I use this one whenever I want to get a good seat on a plane, but you can also use it for attracting a job in aviation.

You will need to gather:

- a small bowl
- 1 teaspoon of sunflower oil
- a silver spoon
- a clean jar with a lid
- 1 teaspoon of jojoba oil
- 2 drops of jasmine essential oil
- 1 chicken stock cube

On the night of a Full Moon, mix together in the bowl the jojoba and sunflower oils and jasmine essential oil with the silver spoon as you concentrate on seeing yourself happily sitting in your favorite seat on the plane or working in your flight attendant's uniform, and repeat this incantation:

'Silver of Mercury my night-time Sun,
in Moonlight's power enchantment has begun.'

Then crumble half the stock cube and sprinkle a little bit into the oil as you say:

'Birds of a feather, I call thee nigh!
With Magic's touch I will soon fly.'

Wipe a tiny bit of the ointment behind your knees and keep the rest of it in the jar.

Universal Compass

This ritual will help you align with the Universal energies and the four cardinal directions wherever you are in the galaxies.

Instead of trying to work out the four directions with a mechanical compass, in your mind's eye imagine instead that your actual body is a compass—with your head North, your right hand East, your feet South and your left hand West.

Stand up straight, with your feet in a comfortable position and with both arms stretched out to either side. Keep the 'body compass' image in mind as you then 'see' the color of pure spiritual white glowing in your North head position. Then 'see' and feel that the color red is glowing warm and vibrant like the Sun in your right hand, which is East, and the color blue is feeling like cool and refreshing water in your left hand in the West, while in the South at your feet, the color brown is helping to 'ground' and connect you with earth. Feel yourself align with the four directions and feel the different temperatures and natures of each of the four colors.

Play around as long as you like with these elements and see how they each give you a different sensation and feeling.

Allow yourself to soar up to the sky with the feeling of white airiness in your mind and then bring this feeling down through to the center of your body, around your stomach area, and bring in some warm color red from your right hand and some of the cool blue from your left hand to do a bit of self-healing and energizing.

When you feel ready to finish your ritual, think about the color brown at your feet in the South, and see how it helps to ground you.

Let yourself finish with a sense that you are now in a place of balance and strength.

ABOUT THE AUTHOR

Deborah Gray was born into a long heritage of Celtic magic and mysticism, and her training as a witch has been an exceptional and, in these modern times, a unique experience. As a teenager she was initiated into one of the world's few remaining Druid Circles. There she was trained by the ancient method of 'magical memory' in the rarely found Oral Tradition of the Craft and began a master's apprenticeship with Australia's most respected occult teacher and witch of the 1970s. She has studied parapsychology and alchemy for over twenty years and is now in her third level of magical mastery. Deborah holds lectures and workshops in metaphysics and spellcasting and is currently exploring the unifying spirit of all magical traditions. Her inspirational words of magic have been translated into seven different languages around the world, and her internationally bestselling books include,
How to Turn your Ex-Boyfriend into a Toad, Nice Girl's Book of Naughty Spells,
How to Turn Your Boyfriend into a Love Slave and
The Mini Book of Love Spells.

Following the Bardic tradition of inspirational song and verse, she is also an award-winning singer/songwriter and has recently recorded a CD of spellbinding jazz music.

To find out more about Deborah Gray's catalog and the fascinating secrets of her coven days as a Sorcerer's Apprentice, log on to her fantastic new website, www.DeborahGray.com where you'll also find 'witch-friendly' message boards, Live Spells, regular Craft news and magical updates for both beginners and experienced witches.
Or go to www.tuttlepublishing.com.

e-mail: info@deborahgray.com